D1083591

the fiesta
system
and
economic
change

the fiesta system and economic change

waldemar r. smith

columbia university press

New York   1977

Waldemar R. Smith is assistant professor of anthropology at the University of Colorado.

The Andrew W. Mellon Foundation, through a special grant, has assisted the Press in publishing this volume.

F
1465.3
.E2
S64

Library of Congress Cataloging in Publication Data

Smith, Waldemar R   1943–
  The fiesta system and economic change.

  Bibliography: p.
  Includes index.
  1. Mayas—Economic conditions.   2. Indians of
Central America—Economic conditions.   3. Mayas—
Rites and ceremonies.   4. Indians of Central
America—Guatemala—Rites and ceremonies.   5. Fasts
and feasts—Guatemala.   I. Title.
F1465.3.E2S64   970'.004'97   77-390
ISBN 0-231-04180-2

Columbia University Press, New York and Guildford, Surrey

for CJE

PREFACE

This is a study of the folk-Catholic fiestas of Maya Indians, and of their role in village and national life. The fiesta system is a topic of considerable interest to Mesoamerican ethnologists, being the institutional locus where major forces in the Indians' spiritual, economic, and political lives intersect and are expressed. In anthropological writings the fiesta system has been variously extolled as a source of Indian cultural continuity, a foundation of village integration, and a bulwark against exploitation. It has also been condemned as an impediment to economic progress and as a mechanism of colonialist control. I attempt in this book to reconcile these viewpoints, and to present new evidence and new analyses of the decline of traditional fiestas in contemporary Mesoamerica.

My fieldwork was carried out in Maya communitites of the highlands of San Marcos, western Guatemala, beginning in August 1968. I spent over two years in the field, in a series of trips. I am grateful to a number of institutions for their support of these expeditions: to the National Institute of Mental Health for a predoctoral fellowship and training grant (MH 11601-01), to the University of California at Santa Barbara for several Patent Fund grants, and to the Council on Research and Creative Work of the University of Colorado for a summer research fellowship. I am also grateful to the University of Colorado Committee on University Scholarly Publications for a publication subvention.

Many individuals provided essential assistance, many more than can be enumerated here. I am especially grateful to Father Daniel Crowe for introducing me to the community of San Miguel Ixtahuacán, and to the Orozco Miranda family for their aid and kind friendship during my stay in San Pedro Sacatepéquez. In Chiapas, Robert Wasserstrom generously lent his time and free use of his new and penetrating analyses of that important Maya region. At

Santa Barbara, James E. Eder, Thomas G. Harding, and John M. Townsend commented enthusiastically and without mercy on my earlier attempts to explain my material. At Boulder, Paul Shankman and William B. Taylor provided the kinds of inspiration that every writer must have: criticism, intellectual companionship, and the highest of scholarly standards. Maria Caliandro and Sally Bates Shankman, tireless editors, did their best to transform my drafts into literate discourse. I am also grateful to Richard D. Basham for his always provocative commentary and other timely aid, and to A. J. Kelso, who, during his tenure as chairman of the Boulder department, provided quiet encouragement and support for the lengthy process of intellectual development that underlies this book.

Finally, deepest thanks go to the two people who have seen this project through from its inception, Linda E. Smith, the companion of all my adventures, and Charles J. Erasmus, my teacher and friend.

W.R.S.
Boulder, November 1976

Contents

Photographs follow page 130

the fiesta system and economic change

ONE

The Fiesta System

In August of 1969, a Guatemalan Indian named Apolinario Miranda sponsored the fiesta of San Augustín, one of the four folk-Catholic festivities celebrated every year in his village. It was his fourth service, the fourth time he had volunteered to host a village ritual. His duties required considerable expenditures of time and resources. Once a week throughout his year of service he was required to refresh the flowers that adorn the altar of San Augustín in the hamlet chapel. In the months before the feast day he set aside corn and beans to feed his guests and money to hire a marimba orchestra for their entertainment. Shortly before the big day he whitewashed his house and slaughtered several fowl and a pig. The feast itself occupied three days of his time, which he passed virtually without sleep. His neighbors offered him little help, for that is not the custom in these villages. Apolinario was the sponsor of the fiesta of San Augustín for 1969 and as sponsor he shouldered the burden of preparation alone.

Apolinario is well-to-do by community standards, and his income—from a tiny store, corn fields, and a small corn mill—is part of the reason for his ceremonial involvement. His community expects that its wealthier members will assume the responsibility of financing village rituals, and Apolinario knows that if he conforms to their wishes his neighbors will respect him and San Augustín will be pleased, while if he is selfish, people will gossip and the saint will withhold his blessing.

Apolinario's fiesta service took place in a modern-day village in a remote corner of Guatemala, but it was similar in form and detail to ceremonies that Indians from Mexico, Guatemala, and the western highlands of South America have been celebrating for some 400 years. Peasant villages throughout the Indian regions of Latin America organize their ritual life on the principle of *mayordomía* or sponsorship. In any community in any year, certain families are appointed stewards (called *cofrades, mayordomos,* or *fiesteros*) of the village saints, and are responsible for the celebrations. After serving for a year they relinquish their posts and responsibilities to new delegates. In the future they may or may not serve again, depending on their inclination, their capacity to sustain the costs of service, and the pressures their neighbors may bring to bear on them.

An outstanding feature of the fiesta system is the extraordinary costs that families bear during their year in office. Fiesta sponsors are expected to hire ritual specialists, perform considerable ceremonial labor, and host a fiesta complete with food, drink, and musical entertainment for other members of the community. Host families generally employ household supplies as far as possible to meet festive budgets, but some items such as sky-rockets and the services of priests and musicians must be purchased with cash.[1] Erasmus (1967:360) has recorded fiesta budgets for communities in two widely separated peasant regions of Latin America. In 16 communities in southeastern Bolivia, household and cash expenditures by sponsoring families were found to vary from $8 to $270, with an average expenditure of $141. In northwest Mexico, variation in 15 communities was from $13 to $246, with an average of $109. In the Maya community of Zinacantán, which has the most elaborate ceremonial organization of any community yet described, a man spends from $4 to over $1100,[2] depending on which of 55 yearly village ceremonial posts he chooses to discharge (Cancian 1965:80). Wolf's summary of the monetary costs shouldered by fiesta sponsor seems apt:

> Evidence from Middle America indicates that a man may have to expend at least the equivalent of one year's local wages to act as a sponsor in a community ceremonial. Expenditures of from two to twenty times this amount are noted for particular communities (1966:7).

These are very large expenditures, especially relative to the low incomes of peasants, but they are not the only costs that mayordomos assume. Fiesta sponsors represent their community before its saints, and thus bear many social responsibilities as well as their heavy financial burden. As temporarily sanctified persons, they are commonly expected to refrain from sexual activity for extended periods of time and to spend hours and days in monotonous ritual. They are also held responsible for the weather, and blamed when it is bad.

Maya Indians believe the saints use the weather as a weapon to punish anyone who mistreats them. Extreme weather is often traced to some transgression or ritual error on the part of mayordomos. In Santiago Chimaltenango, for example, sponsoring a fiesta

is not only expensive to the incumbent, but *muy delicado* (very delicate or dangerous). Sins, either of omission or commission, on the part of *mayordomos* reflect on the village, bringing down the anger of Santiago or *Dios* upon the whole populace. They must not neglect the saints, forget a saint's day, or omit regular prayers and offerings of candles. It was the fault of the First *Mayordomo* when, several years ago, Santiago caused rains to wash out the market on the Fiesta of Santiago (Wagley 1949:83; see also Guiteras-Holmes 1961:93).

The Indians' explanation for the rainfall was that

the *mayordomos* did not offer Santiago his customary drink and he was not drunk during the fiesta. He was irritated at the noise people made during the fiesta, so he caused rain to fall and wash away the displays of merchandise in the plaza. "It was the fault of the *mayordomos*" (Wagley 1949:83-84n).

Weather is unpredictable, and the possibility is great that sometime during the complex rituals the mayordomo will break a taboo or commit some other error. Bad weather can always be blamed on the sponsors, whose punishment then serves to square accounts with the saint. This often results in mayordomos being thrown in jail. In an early ethnological survey of Guatemala, Rosales visited San Mateo Ixtatán, and was told by the local Ladino official that

at times he orders the encarceration of the principal indigenous prayermakers of the community when there is bad weather; he does this at the request of the Indians of the place, because according to their beliefs the prayermakers are at fault when there are heavy rains or strong winds. Their transgression is that they sleep with their wives during the year that they hold the *cargo* of rezador. They spend one or two days and nights in jail, or until they themselves ask to be let out when the weather breaks. Once released, they head for the mountain peaks to make their costumbres in request of good weather (Goubaud Carrera, Rosales, and Tax 1947:24).

My original purpose in writing this book was to analyze the fiesta system as a case of nonproductive consumption in peasant society. Previous studies provide detailed descriptions of the fiesta systems of many communities. From them we know that folk rituals are a central part of village life, and that a man's position in the community is determined to a large degree by his ritual participation. I wanted to go beyond these descriptions to questions of the motivations behind fiesta sponsorship and its wider social significance. Specifically, I wanted to know under what conditions people would support the fiesta system with its heavy personal costs, and under what conditions they would switch to more economic and individualistic forms of consumption. I also wanted to know how religious spending relates to the Indians' position in national society, and whether fiesta consumption is really an important cause of Indian social and cultural insularity, as it is so often portrayed to be.

Answering these questions, however, led me to broader topics. According to my analysis, the fiesta system is less a cause of the Indians' cultural and social status than a consequence of how Indians have been integrated into Mesoamerican colonial regimes. Exclusion of Indians from cosmopolitan social life, coupled with their subjugated economic position and their freedom in running their own community affairs, are the larger conditions that motivate fiesta sponsorship. As this pattern of integration changes—and it is doing so in a number of ways in contemporary Guatemala—fiesta systems tend to be replaced by radically different forms of ritual participation. The study of ritual and ritual change thus involves the larger question of the changing relationships between local Indian communities and national society, making the description and explanation of social change in the Guatemalan countryside another major goal of this study.

Analyzing Guatemalan social change gave rise in turn to a third, theoretical, question. Functionalist interpretations of the fiesta system depict it as the keystone of Indian life. The Indians' emotional and financial commitment to the fiesta system, so the argument goes, inhibits Ladinoization and preserves the Indian lifestyle. This explanation of Indian cultural stability is similar to several recent "plural society" and "ecological" analyses of Mesoamerican ethnicity—as well as to more general theories that attribute ongoing poverty to the achievement needs, cognitive orientation, or culture of the poor. All these theories concentrate more attention on the mental and ideological characteristics of the poor than on the objective position of poor people in the broader society. Sometimes they go so far as to imply that poor communities limit themselves; their stagnant position is held to result from their world view or religious values.

I will show that in the case at hand these ideological perspectives would lead to a neglect of crucial national-level political forces, important local conditions and resources, and the complex interaction of these factors that in fact determines stability and change in Indian communities. The case of the fiesta system strongly implies that Indian symbolic culture does affect the ethnic *status quo,* but in a derivative way. Given the resistance of outside society, Indians have elaborated and maintained an alternative lifestyle that provides a variety of human gratifications, but does so at the expense of group coordination and capacity for change. Despite its substantiation of social boundaries, however, this lifestyle is first and foremost a response to those boundaries, and its major features, such as fiesta systems, can disappear with remarkable speed when Indian communities begin to experience significant economic changes.

I undertook this study in the highlands of the Department of San Marcos, a predominantly Indian region of western Guatemala. Orthodox Catholicism has never been strong in this area, and the people have developed complex systems of folk-Catholic ritual to fulfill their spiritual and social needs. Until recently, fiestas were an integral part of all these systems.

The socioeconomic structure of this region has changed markedly, however, in recent years. Markets and educational opportunities have expanded, transportation systems are becoming more extensive and efficient, new productive capital has become available, the population has grown, and much of the population is involved in seasonal plantation labor. These developments have not affected the entire region uniformly. Some communities have been affected beneficially, some detrimentally, and others hardly at all. The processes of change are numerous, and they interact in various ways to produce what is more a mosaic than a pattern; this mosaic is very difficult to characterize in unambiguous generalizations. Thus the broad statements that follow are made with caution.

One fairly clear trend is that traditional, sponsored ceremonials are becoming increasingly inappropriate to the changing world of western Guatemalans. Village fiesta organizations are weakening or collapsing everywhere—though at quite different rates from community to community. People in highland San Marcos in general wish to reduce the individual costs of ceremonial participation. The incentives behind conspicuous giving have weakened everywhere, promoting considerable experimentation with ritual forms.

The result has been the recent elaboration of three new types of ceremonial organization in many of the communities of the region—a kind of institutional adaptive radiation. I shall refer to these types as *truncated, appended,* and *administered* ceremonial organizations. All have developed as organizational tactics to reduce individual costs of ritual.

The first tactic occurs where people choose to reduce costs by "truncating" or simplifying their fiestas, as one community did when it reduced the festivities for its patron saint from a yearly cycle of four fiestas to a single annual event. Another tactic has been to preserve the traditional opulence of fiestas but to increase the number of sponsors responsible for each event, thus reducing the average individual contribution. This is the "appended" option. The most radical new ceremonial form that I observed occurs where the sponsorship principle has been abandoned altogether, and ceremonies have become the lasting responsibility of special, permanent-membership groups. In some instances these groups are no more than ad hoc committees, while in others they are large brotherhoods (some with hundreds of members) that enjoy formal status within the orthodox Church. In either case, "administered" organizations distribute festive costs over a large number of people through collections or through fund-raising promotions, the proceeds of which are disbursed by the officials of the group.

Of the three new types, administered organizations appear to be the most difficult to establish successfully. In San Marcos these organizations have been modeled along the lines of the Holy Week *hermandades* (brotherhoods) of the urban people of Quezaltenango, Antigua, and Guatemala City, and occur only in those communities that have developed significant contact with national society and culture.

We might, in guarded generalization, define two major trends of change in rural Guatemala, both of which are altering the socioeconomic integration of local communities with the national society. On the one hand, some communities are becoming too poor to support themselves, even at their customary simple level of living. Investigators now discuss with increasing frequency what is called the "subfamily farm" in rural Guatemala, which no longer supports the family that owns it. This trend is associated with high rates of population growth not accompanied by agrarian development or local emigration, and its consequence is that many communities have lost their subsistence autonomy and have become highly dependent on seasonal wage labor on coffee, cotton, or sugar plantations. A few Indian communities, on the other hand, have lost their independence in the more beneficial direction of economic growth. These are the major centers of Indian entrepreneurship and modernization in western Guatemala—towns that have entered a stage of self-sustaining development.

I began my research in San Miguel Ixtahuacán, a township of small farmers and seasonal laborers. San Miguel is a remote interior mountain community with a highly Indian culture. But its isolation and conservatism notwithstanding, the community has modified its ceremonial organizations in significant ways over the last few decades. The causes of this modification have been the intensifying subsistence crisis of the interior mountains plus recent religious and political changes.

Having seen what increasing poverty can do to sponsored ceremonies, I became curious about the impact of increasing affluence. I therefore moved to San Pedro, the *cabecera* (head town) of the township of San Pedro Sacatepéquez. San Pedro is a bustling Indian town enjoying unprecedented prosperity. Here I also found that a previously strong system of sponsored ceremonials was in a state of collapse, and was being supplanted by new types of organization. It appears that sponsored ceremonial organizations are viable only between economic limits, having a lower limit of poverty and an upper limit of affluence.

For a control population I then sought out two communities that are still ceremonially conservative. These are San Pedro Petz, an isolated but fairly prosperous peasant hamlet belonging to the township of Sacatepéquez, and the small neighboring town of San Cristóbal Cucho. Compared to other regional communities, these two have been relatively successful in maintaining an economically independent way of life and in preserving much of their traditional ceremonial life.

Since it is now difficult to find communities in San Marcos with full-blown fiesta systems, chapter 2 collates historical and ethnographic materials to provide a general background on the role this institution has played in a colonial society. Chapters 3 and 4 then take a critical look at the functionalist interpretation of the fiesta system, using the well-documented case of Zinacantán, in the highlands of Chiapas, Mexico. Chapters 5 and 6 provide background on the highlands of San Marcos and on the traditional ritual organization of the communities studied. Chapters 7 through 10 outline recent socioeconomic changes in San Miguel Ixtahuacán and San Pedro, and chapters 11 to 13 trace the effects of these changes on fiesta motivation and the organization of public ritual. Since there is little ethnography on either proletarian Indian communities or modernizing Indian communities, I have attempted to supply as much detail as possible in these chapters. The concluding chapter attempts to explain, from the perspectives of politics, wealth, and ethnic competition, the socioeconomic changes that are disrupting fiesta systems in the communities of San Marcos.

Notes

[1]In some Mesoamerican communities, *cofradías* hold property or run enterprises, the proceeds of which are used to finance ceremonies. For example, the cofradía of Santo Tomás, the patron saint of Chichicastenango, sells meat in the plaza and operates small dance salons to obtain funds (Bunzel 1967:169; see Taylor 1972:71, 169-70 for cofradía property in colonial Oaxaca). Where they occur, such enterprises reduce the sponsor's material outlay, though they still require that he donate considerable labor.

[2]This figure represents the total expenditure made by the man who served Senior Mayordomo Rey in the Zinacantán hierarchy in 1960. It is the largest sponsor-borne expenditure ever recorded for a Mesoamerican fiesta (Cancian 1965:81).

TWO

A Political Perspective

In their fascination for Indian ceremonial life, anthropologists have put forward three important interpretations of the fiesta system. The most common of these is based on the functionalist idea that village rituals provide Indians with a kind of cultural "insulation" that protects them from being acculturated into the national mainstream. Another, more Marxian, view is that the fiesta system was imposed on Indians by colonial states in order to drain off resources, control labor, and fragment Indian populations into politically weak villages. A third, colonialist, perspective finds Indian tradition (especially ritual tradition) and colonial opression to stand in a mutual, symbiotic relationship that shores up and stabilizes the larger society in both its colonial and its colonized elements. There is support for all three of these positions, and an element of truth in each, but none provides a complete picture. Each, in its partial way, fails to answer one or the other of the critical questions that are the topic of this chapter:

1. What motivates Indians to allocate scarce resources to religious spending?
2. What effect does the pattern of religious integration that results from this consumption have on the Indians' status in colonial society?

The common functionalist interpretation depicts fiestas as positive features in Indian village life. In the functionalist view, the fiesta system is the central element in village social structure—it strengthens village cohesion by providing core values and insulating the community against acculturation. Stressing the village-level benefits of the fiesta system, functionalists usually describe it as part of a native "prestige economy," which Indians by and large support voluntarily (Adams 1957; Cancian 1965; Nash 1958, 1966:35-36; Tax 1953; Vogt 1969:246-71). The problem with the functionalist interpretation is that it answers neither of the above questions. However true it is that the fiesta system is a key institution in village life, the idea that it is also an insulator makes any analysis of regional processes unnecessary, and any understanding of fiesta motivation impossible.

Some anthropologists have attempted to put the idea of insulation into a broader context by arguing that the fiesta system levels wealth and thus solidifies the village against exploitation rather than acculturation (Wolf 1967). This is a stronger interpretation in that it provides the institution with an adaptive rationale and clearly recognizes the Indian villagers' need to cope actively with a powerful outside world. The Marxist critique of this position is that as a defense against exploitation the fiesta system is notably ineffective, and furthermore the positive emphasis on prestige and adaptation does not account for the system's coercive features (Harris 1964:25-35; Nuñez del Prado 1955). According to this critique, the fiesta system was never really an Indian institution at all, and Indians supported it only because they were coerced by non-Indian authorities.

The colonialist interpretation is more elaborate yet, viewing village fiestas not simply as a willful imposition by outsiders, but as a part of a balanced, mutually supportive interplay between national pressure and village interest. According to Favre (1973), this interplay of colonial politics and Indian culture allows us to understand how ethnic groups within Chiapas society can express simultaneously ''a pretension of autonomy and a talent for interdependence.'' The Indian, Favre says, lives in a ''community,'' a complexly woven society designed to produce *people,* in contrast to Ladino society, which is organized to produce wealth. The Indian social model rejects reigning Ladino values of accumulation, and the inequality it fosters, basing itself instead on solidarity and equality, which are preserved by self-stabilizing leveling mechanisms such as the fiesta system. Favre gives as an example of the colonial wedding of tradition and exploitation the observation that in Chiapas the most intensely Indian communities are found closest to the center of Ladino power. Chamula, the Indian community most involved in plantation labor, also has the most elaborate folk ceremonials. As colonial pressures become more threatening to their solidarity, Favre argues, Indian communities respond by augmenting control over their members, especially ritual control of economic surpluses. This has the simultaneous effect of entrenching the Indians' traditional communitarian adaptation while cutting them off from the alternative adaptation of economic mobility.

Favre's basic point is well taken, that the fiesta system helps maintain the status quo by stabilizing both sectors of colonial society, but the mechanism he develops is inconsistent with an array of ethnographic facts. The fiesta system does not, for example, level wealth, which implies that its major effects do not lie in the area of wealth control. Furthermore, comparable forms of ritualized giving are commonly found in isolated tribal societies, which implies that the impetus behind such giving does not necessarily develop as a defensive response to exploitation.

This chapter shows that the fiesta system is part of a colonial ecology, in that the exclusion of Indians from metropolitan social and economic life creates the conditions in which the fiesta system can thrive, while the fiesta system in turn substantiates the superiority of the metropolitan society. The motivation behind ritual giving appears, however, to arise from economic rather than political logic, while its broader impact appears to be in the Indians' political rather than their economic capacities.

The Fiesta System as Contributor to Colonialism

After the Conquest, Spanish colonists were faced with the problem of controlling and utilizing large Indian populations. In essence, the Spaniards' problem was how to incorporate the conquered Indians into their economy without pushing them over the brink of revolt. Accomplishing this required that the Spaniards keep the Indians (who everywhere outnumbered them by sizable margins) in a state of relative disorganization. They quickly developed a talent for this task. Their military conquests were originally successful because of the adroit way in which they pitted Indian confederacies against one another, a divide-and-conquer strategy they followed consistently in Mexico, Yucatan, Guatemala, and Peru (Samayoa Chinchilla 1960). The "bottomless triangles" of patronage were a later variation on the same theme, where the peons related to the patron individually rather than collectively. An Indian society based on village-level organization likewise contributed to this end because, however numerous the Indians, so long as they were fragmented into autonomous villages they were less threatening to the colonial state.

The fiesta system, as the basis of Indian social organization, was thus politically useful to Spanish society. It provided Indians with personal satisfactions, as well as being a source of religious belief and of harmless social competition. More important, it was an institution that produced leaders, interests, and organizations that were strictly local, turning Indian villages in on themselves rather than out toward one another (Harris 1964:29-30). In so doing, the fiesta system supported the colonial status quo by contributing to the relative disorganization of Indian society. This could be why the Spaniards tolerated Indian folk religion despite their avowed concern for spreading the true faith.

The problem of controlling the Indians was particularly acute in colonial Chiapas and Guatemala. The conquest of Central America was bloodier and more protracted than that of central Mexico. Central America was attacked from two sides by competing, uncoordinated armies who encountered a series of petty kingdoms that had to be conquered piecemeal. After the Conquest, tribute, taxation, and relocations produced a climate of ethnic tension, broken by occasional storms of Indian protest. This protest was potentially so dangerous that, despite chronic shortages of labor, many colonists resisted the importation of slaves for fear of revolts (Jones 1940:9-10; MacLeod 1973:41-43, 52, 191, 212-13). This problem was all the more severe because Mesoamerica attracted far fewer Spaniards than the gold-rich regions of central Mexico and Peru. Despite their grievances and their superior numbers, however, the Indians never succeeded in eliminating Spanish control. A close look at the Tzeltal rebellion of 1712, the most violent uprising in the Maya highlands, helps explain why.

At that time the highlands of Chiapas were dominated by the royal city of San Cristóbal de Las Casas, whose residents lived off the labor and agriculture of surrounding Indian villages (Klein 1966). Spanish merchants in San Cristóbal charged the Indians exorbitant prices, while civil authorities impoverished them with trumped-up legal charges and drawn-out trials. The church could be as bad or worse. Just before the Tzeltal rebellion, an avaricious bishop proceeded to enrich himself by swinging through the countryside taxing Indian communities. His first *visita* was very costly to the Indians. On the day he began his second one, 28 Tzeltal townships joined in a pact of war and killed every Spaniard caught in their territory.

The Tzeltal rebellion was based on Indian religious integration and was preceded by an intense religious movement. As early as 1708 an "insane Ladino hermit" had gained considerable control over Indians on the outskirts of San Cristóbal, so threatening the authorities that they jailed him, declared him possessed, and ultimately sent him to his death in exile. This hardly solved the Spaniards' problems, since immediately after the hermit was gone the Indians were seized by a series of miraculous appearances of the Virgin. The authorities moved again, attempting to burn the Virgin's shrine, but were rebuffed by the Indians. By this time the Indian movement had developed a central leadership (which included Lucas Pérez, a wealthy Tzeltal who had been ruined by Spanish chicanery), and the Virgin's messages had become openly revolutionary—urging the Indians to "kill all the priests and curates as well as Spaniards, Mestizos, Negroes, and Mulattoes" (Klein 1966:225). The Tzeltals rapidly expanded the civil-religious hierarchies of their communities into a single hierarchy embracing the whole linguistic group. They appointed priests, established a treasury, and with an army of 4000 moved on San Cristóbal.

The history of Chiapas displays the typical colonial dialectic of ongoing exploitation punctuated by occasional revolt. When circumstances welded the scattered Indians into an insurrectionary force, as they did in 1712, the exploiters had to fall back on force of arms to maintain their position. As the Tzeltal rebels moved toward San Cristóbal, they were stalled by a military force one-quarter their size, giving the Spaniards time to call in reinforcements from Guatemala. Once these were on the field, the issue was quickly settled, with superior weapons giving the Spaniards a critical advantage. In the final battle, the Indians, fighting with farm implements, had 1000 casualties. The Spaniards suffered 200 wounded, one dead.

Superior organization, however, was more critical to the Spanish triumph than superior weapons. While local Spaniards called on the Council of the Indies and quickly summoned reinforcements from as far away as Guatemala, the Tzeltals, lacking such coordination, failed to convince even their Tzotzil neighbors to join the struggle. Tzeltal revolutionary politics, like their everyday politics, were inspired by religion and based on an expanded ad hoc version of village institutions. These institutions proved so inadequate that as a revolutionary movement and alternative government the Tzeltal "republic" lasted less than a year. Even at its best, Indian religious cohesion was no match for concentrated Spanish power.

The Spaniards viewed Indian hostility as an established fact and a matter of gravest concern—It was not defense of doctrine that inspired the authorities' attempt to nip the Tzeltal religious movement in the bud. So deep was the Spaniards' fear of the Indian masses that the Council of the Indies spent the large sum of 65,000 pesos to suppress the Tzeltal uprising, and the Guatemalan reinforcements that crushed the Indian army were led by the president of Guatemala himself. The Spaniards were more worried about their dominance and knew that preserving it by physical force was disruptive and expensive. It was thus to their advantage to allow the Indians any practice that reduced their cohesion as a social class. Only in this way could they offset the Indians' numerical superiority, reduce the threat of revolt, and ensure that revolts, when they did occur, would be contained at a manageable, local stage. The fiesta system, which reinforced and deepened the fragmentation of Indian society into a series of culturally self-sufficient and politically ineffective communities, fitted this need perfectly. As long as Indian life was structured at the village level only, the Spaniards had less to fear—and this measure of control, unlike military confrontation, was free.

The Fiesta System as Response to Colonialism

Besides debilitating the Indians politically, the fiesta system drained Indian money into the hands of colonial priests and merchants. Priests, who depended on parish tithes and stipends for their support, promoted ritual activity among their Indian parishoners (Harris 1964). Manufacturers of candles, fireworks, and other ritual items also profited from Indian fiestas. Even today an entire Ladino neighborhood in San Cristóbal specializes in the production and sale of ritual goods.

The fiesta system did not, however, level Indian wealth, as it is commonly held to have done (Nash 1958, 1966:35-36; Tax 1953; Van Zantwijk 1967:246; Wolf 1959:216). The leveling hypothesis maintains that richer Indians become poorer when they sponsor fiestas, and this in turn increases village solidarity by reducing economic distinctions between villagers and suppressing social mobility.

If the fiesta system actually operated like this, economic leveling would be yet another way that colonial society benefited from Indian religion. The problem is that economic leveling, to be truly effective, would entail redistribution of productive capital within the village, and this does not occur as a result of religious sponsorship. Fiestas are periods of heightened consumption; they are not a forum for providing land, animals, or any other source of income to poorer villagers. Furthermore, *fiesteros* I studied never sponsored fiestas out of accumulated wealth-on-hand (see also Cancian 1965:100-103). They made a concentrated effort to collect the necessary reserves (usually by increasing household productivity and cutting household costs) *after* they accepted office. "This is why cofrades are always appointed in advance," one man explained, "so they will have time to save."

Much of the wealth expended in festive service would not have come into sponsors' hands were it not for their religious obligations, which implies that the fiesta system is a savings motivator more than a savings leveler. Shifting the emphasis this way—from the consequences of religious spending to its motivating causes—leads us to new questions: What are the specific inducements that prompt Indian peasants to spend so much on religion? More important, what are the broader social conditions that make these inducements effective and powerful in the context of Indian life?[1] The answer, as we shall see, is that religious spending is a logical, economic response in a society that is: (1) excluded from effective participation in the market, (2) given considerable freedom to run its own cultural affairs, and (3) relegated to a rural, village existence. The fiesta system, in short, is an institutionalized reaction by Indians to the way they were economically, politically, and socially incorporated into the colonial state.

At the village level, the fiesta system is simultaneously a coercive and a voluntary organization. It is coercive because it is everywhere backed by strong social pressures that make it difficult for people to avoid their religious duties. Historically, priests often simply assigned men to office, and their orders were not to be disobeyed. Village mayors and *principales* (elders) also forced service by applying moral pressure and threatening people with jail. Vestiges of such official coercion can still be found in Guatemala, especially in remote communities. The community at large also prods people to live up to expectations by subjecting reluctant individuals to vicious gossip (Cancian 1965:98; Reina 1966:124). Forced service even occurs in contemporary Zinacantán, though the Zinacantán case shows that the voluntary incentive of prestige-striving is also an important source of fiestero motivation. With its 55 yearly posts, Zinacantán has the most elaborate and expensive fiesta system of any known community. Some of these posts cost hundreds of dollars to discharge, yet many Zinacantecos support their fiesta system so zealously that the community recently had to begin keeping a written record of the men who had volunteered their services. The more popular and expensive posts are reserved for the next 20 years. Prestige-striving is the major stimulus to this festive competition (Cancian 1963, 1965:86-96).

There is no contradiction in this co-occurrence of coercive and voluntary incentives. Gossip and political power are used universally by small communities to enforce their norms. Such communities also tend to have vigorous internal prestige systems, since life in little villages is so public that people naturally engage in continuous mutual evaluation and ranking. In such situations the logical way for a man to stand out is to make a dramatic personal sacrifice in support of village ideals. Wealthier people are thus doubly motivated to be socially conscious. They know the village expects them to be publicly active and will punish reluctance; they also know that their contributions will ultimately be repaid with intense displays of gratitude and deference. In Mesoamerican villages these displays include constant toasting, embracing, and recognition of fiesteros with titles and positions of honor (Guiteras-Holmes 1961:72-73; Mendelsohn 1957:133; Nash 1958:67-68; Vogt 1969:238-41). The ranking mayordomos of Chichicastenango, in Bunzel's description, are a near-regal body, with vast powers over community life and numerous privileges, such as the right to carry silver scepters (1967:168). Village elders who earned their status through public service are the ''zenith'' of power and moral authority in Santiago Chimaltenango (Wagley 1949:85). In Chenalhó, people even believe that the more important sponsors are infused with supernatural grace, and personify the deities they serve (Guiteras-Holmes 1961:97).

Coercion and prestige oddly but naturally coexist as ritual inducements in Indian communities. Coercion, however, seems to vary in intensity, both historically and according to the economic circumstances of villages. Guatemalan fiesta systems have recently become much less coercive because rural villages are now more closely tied to national politics. Traditional leaders, such as the principales, have lost their power, party affiliation has replaced ritual status as the source of village power, and people have learned that local government cannot legally enforce religious participation. Official coercion is also more common in poorer Indian communities, where sponsorship is a greater economic burden, than in relatively prosperous places such as Zinacantán (see chapter 4).

The important—and often neglected—point is that these positive and negative rewards are effective at the village level *only* because of the Indians' position in the larger society. Indians were incorporated into the colonial economy as suppliers of food and labor. Being peasants, they find it relatively easy to accumulate occasional surpluses. They are forced to purchase some ritual goods, but the major festive item, food, is produced by the family, and this home production helps reduce the felt costs of ritual feasting. More important, from the very beginning the Indians have been excluded from the progressive, dynamic sector of the colonial market. Commercial farming, mining, and manufacturing have been almost totally a Spanish preserve. This exclusion from the investment sector, in conjunction with the stagnation of the Indians' own peasant farming, is the fundamental precondition of festive consumption.

Throughout the world, wherever we find people giving away wealth in a customary and ritualized fashion to establish status, we find a premarket situation—for example, in the Trobriand Islands, in village India, on the northwest coast of North America, or in Mesoamerica. Ritual consumption tends to occur where economies are rural and traditional, rather than urban and dynamic, and where people are not subject to the investor-consumer pressures of the market. Remote tribesmen, peasants, or any socially isolated group have comparatively few other uses for the time and surpluses they consume ritually. Market isolation thus reduces the felt costs of public consumption, and at the same time opens the way for social incentives such as gossip and prestige allocation.

Both the coercive and voluntary inducements behind Indian religious feasting are further strengthened by the political and social aspects of Indian colonial status. The indirect rule of Spanish colonialism allowed Indian communities considerable freedom to run their own affairs and enforce their own customs. Were it not for this feature of Indian political status, Indian leaders would not have enjoyed the autonomy to coerce ritual participation.

Village prestige systems likewise arose from the social isolation of Indian communities. Because of discrimination and exclusion from cosmopolitan Spanish society, Indians had few opportunities for mobility or personal gratification outside their villages. This isolation and village dependence enhanced the importance of local prestige and local reputation, making validation of community status a vital personal need.

Such a pattern of Indian integration, featuring strong economic restrictions and social exclusion, along with a degree of political autonomy, involved the Indians in a situation where public generosity could be strongly rewarded and selfishness stringently punished, and where other possibilities for "turning a profit" were few. Within these constraints, ritual giving is predictable.

Indian Commitment and Ritual Change

Given the stagnant, rural Indian society under Mesoamerican colonialism, the tendency toward conspicuous giving was natural enough to make the fiesta system an economically rational institution. This does not mean, however, that people were totally and uniformly committed to it. The fiesta system meshed with its economic surroundings in such a way that the opportunity costs of sponsorship were relatively low, but sponsors still had to face sexual abstinence, responsibility for the weather, and the additional work and worry that came with their public position. Indians consequently have always referred to their ritual organizations as *cargo* (burden) or ''work service'' systems, and have been known to make active efforts to avoid service (Cancian 1965:131, 185; Erasmus, 1961:272; Wagley 1949:89-96). Public resistance is found even in conservative communities such as Zinacantán, which may mean that it is an inherent, universal feature of the fiesta system.

In some cases, Indians are so disinvolved in their community religious life that they try to put it to personal use. This occurred in a Oaxacan village when an influential man, in league with the local clergy, began making poor villagers accept cargos they could not afford. Through a series of loans and foreclosures, this man and a few other creditor families were able to gain control of more than 90 percent of the village's land (Flannery 1972:415). A similar case occurred in the Guatemalan village of Agua Escondida, when a group of sharp outsiders accumulated capital for a loan operation by establishing a new fiesta financed out of community collections (Redfield 1945:267). In both cases, people consciously manipulated ritual financing in order to turn a monetary profit.

Even under traditional conditions, people approach the fiesta system with varying attitudes, including cynicism (Saler 1971:339, 1972:202; Vogt 1972). The variability in individual motivation can also be seen in cases of contemporary sponsorship. Apolinario Miranda, who introduced this study, sponsors fiestas in part to enhance his status, in part because his village accepts cofradía service as an alternative to civil service, which he fears because of its legal complexities. Chepe Aguilar of Subchal has sponsored two fiestas, the first because he was forced, the second, under a less costly arrangement, out of sincere social and religious commitment. Daniel González of Chamac sponsors feasts primarily because he is so concerned with his village status, while his neighbor Angela Orozco, who is marginally involved with village society, recently rescued the faltering fiesta of Chamac out of intense devotion to the native religion.

The economic situation of peasant Indians did not eliminate the burden of sponsorship altogether, or the resistance this burden often inspired. It did, however, minimize the opportunity costs of ceremonial giving. At the same time, the autonomous and isolated character of Indian villages provided strong communal incentives toward public-spirited sacrifice. These incentives, in conjunction with the economic milieu, created a motivational balance strong enough to overcome most individual reluctance, providing the fiesta system with the kind of support it has needed to survive through four centuries of Mesoamerican history. The irony is that this village-level web of pressures, rewards, and types of involvement, however "genuine" it seems as the bedrock of Indian culture, is first and foremost a response to the pattern of opportunities imposed from without on the conquered, subjugated Indians. The fiesta system is part of an ecology of colonial control because it is Indian in its ideology, participants, and motivation, but is ultimately perpetuated by an outside world that benefits from its existence.

Notes

[1]My analytic strategy here is based on the Barnard-Simon theory of organizational equilibrium. The basic idea of this theory is that the objectives of a collective activity (such as a village fiesta system) are not necessarily congruent with the goals of its participants, but if the collectivity is to survive, the two must be related. The success or "equilibrium" of any organization depends on continued participation. This can be achieved only if the organization can provide its participants with goal-satisfying inducements which, in their perception, are at least as valuable as the contributions the organization asks them to make (see Barnard 1966:13; Barrett 1970; March and Simon 1958:84-85).

THREE

Functionalism and the Fiesta System: The Case of Zinacantán

Ritual generosity is less a human virtue than a matter of opportunity. In little communities with stable, traditional economies, people are often quite generous, not despite the scarcity of their material wealth but because of it. Scarcity puts a premium on generosity, sometimes for reasons of survival, always for reasons of prestige. In Guatemalan villages generosity takes the form of folk-Catholic feasting, in which peasants can earn what is for them magnificent social acclaim while giving up surpluses of small alternative utility. As we shall see, when communities fall on hard times, surpluses are difficult to create, and these communities often economize on ritual feasting. In prosperous, developing communities surpluses are abundant, but their possible uses are even more so; and in these communities, we shall also see that people reduce the range of their generosity. Both kinds of economic change alter the value of surpluses and pave the way for new kinds of ritual organization.

The preceding paragraph summarizes one of the theses of this book and also the current state of the fiesta system in western Guatemala. As an interpretation of fiesta economics, however, it is at odds with the prevailing view in Mesoamerican anthropology. The mainstream interpretation of the fiesta system is that religious generosity is a cause of Indian social and economic stability, rather than a consequence of that stability. The conventional interpretation depicts the fiesta system as a kind of gyroscope in the social system of the little community. It presents ritual giving as a defensive prestige economy that provides "insulation" against the outside capitalist world and preserves the Indian lifeway. From this perspective, festive giving not only is divorced from any analysis of the Indians' position in the broader society, but is portrayed as the very mechanism that divorces them from that society. Since my contention is just the opposite, a discussion of the conventional interpretation is in order.

We can best assess the issue through analysis of Cancian's studies of Zinacantán, especially his first book, *Economics and Prestige in a Maya Community*. These studies make a good focus because they deal with a well-studied region of Mexico and provide abundant material for alternative analysis. Cancian's work is also useful because it is the only book-length treatment of a community fiesta system and, more importantly, because it makes explicit the functionalist orientation that underlies all the conventional interpretations.

The major topic of Cancian's first book is not fiestas per se, but ethnic boundaries, and how fiestas maintain the gap between the inner Indian world and external Mexican society. Its central argument is that the fiesta or cargo system of Zinacantán integrates and preserves the Indian community, and that major culture change will not occur until the cargo system breaks down. This is a functionalist argument of that organismic variety that portrays communities as unified, harmonic systems that seek their own equilibrium through exclusively internal processes. This organicism is its principal weakness. The conventional interpretation fails to explain either festive giving or ethnic boundaries precisely because it is based on the functionalist cliché that community culture can be understood without reference to the surrounding world.

Zinacantán, home of some 15,000 Maya peasants, lies in the mountains of Chiapas, in southern Mexico. It is actually a township, similar in its topography and dispersed settlement pattern to Guatemalan municipios such as San Miguel Ixtahuacán. Zinacantecos subsist primarily from subsistence farming and plaza trade. Most are illiterate. They speak Tzotzil as their first, and in some cases only, language. They are folk Catholics, maintaining an unusually rich ceremonial and cosmological culture without the aid of a resident priest. They are highly endogamous. They tend to be suspicious of outsiders and occasionally hostile; only the barest handful of Ladinos live in their community. They even wear a unique costume that distinguishes them from Ladinos and from other rural Indians. But, for all their tribal uniqueness, they are not isolated from outside society because they live only a short walk from the city of San Cristóbal, which they visit regularly.

The human variety of highland Chiapas is extraordinary; the numerous rural Indian communities, each with its unique dress and dialect, blanket the region like a cultural crazy quilt. All are in turn lorded over by the 25,000 residents of San Cristóbal, whose elite represents the culture, money, and power of modern Mexico. For Zinacantán and its neighbors, San Cristóbal is a major connection with the outside world, but it is a community that has always accepted Indians as peasants only. Ethnic interaction in Chiapas is tightly patterned and restricted; the city dominates the countryside, Ladinos dominate Indians, and now, as always, there is little mobility into the middle and upper Ladino ranks. This differentiation of power and privilege is the key to understanding highland Chiapas, which is more than an area of "plural societies," of ethnic groups that interact but do not meld. Society in Chiapas is a stratified regional organization, the basic feature of which, hidden under the colorful veneer of native costume and customs, is a grossly inegalitarian system of social class.

The Harvard Chiapas Project has studied the region for almost two decades but has paid little attention to this overarching pattern of class and power. The project, in fact, might be more aptly titled the Zinacantán Project, since its primary interest has been in the culture of this single community, where it has maintained at least one investigator in the field continuously since 1960. Such focused ethnography cannot be justified in a stratified, multiethnic society because it leads to neglect of the forest out of fascination for a single tree. We might suspect that the intense Indianness of Zinacantán, which its investigators so admire, is produced and maintained to a significant degree by the severe liabilities imposed on peasants by powerful urban Ladinos. We shall not know for sure, however, so long as the investigators treat the community as if it were a cultural island. Vogt's *Zinacantan*, a monumental community study which collates the work done by some 90 project affiliates over a dozen years, epitomizes this ethnographic tendency. Although a mine of information on the community, the book presents no systematic treatment of Zinacantán's position in the Chiapas class system. In this 695-page text Ladinos are mentioned on 32 scattered pages.

Cancian's work is one of the main products of the project's research and reflects its dominant interest in noncomparative community ethnography. This interest is perhaps responsible for the disagreement between his conclusions and mine. In studying a stable community from the inside, Cancian found organismic functionalism to be the most convenient model for interpreting his material and, once adopted, this model offered further rationale for neglecting larger social relations. In this chapter and the following one, I shall show that the impact of the outside world is as essential to an understanding of Zinacantán as to its Guatemalan counterparts, that the community's cargo system is more a creature than a cause of social boundaries, and that it is already in the process of breaking down as the Indians' status changes in response to regional development.

Discussion centers on two issues. One is the theoretical issue of whether institutions should be considered causes of behavior or whether they are simply the sociologist's abstraction from behavior's patterned expression. My position is that when environmental conditions (the broader natural, demographic, and social factors that surround individuals and groups) are stable for any length of time, communities learn to cope with them in standard ways, so their behavior assumes patterns we conceptualize as institutions. Functionalism turns this abstraction into an explanation, and gives it precedence over the environment that created it.

The second issue concerns an alternative explanation for ritual giving and ethnic boundaries in Chiapas. Here we need to explain why Zinacantecos support such an elaborate and costly fiesta system, and why this system is presently changing. This chapter deals with the first issue, the following chapter with the second.

The Functionalist View of the Cargo System

The cargo system of Zinacantán is the most elaborate communal ritual organization of any Latin American peasant community studied to date. There are 55 yearly posts in Zinacantán, so many that virtually all Zinacateco men participate, and some participate several times. Cancian estimates that about 90 percent of the men in the community sponsor at least one fiesta, a situation that he refers to as *full participation*. The fact of full participation indicates that the community is still strongly committed to traditional ritual. Since the beginning of the century Zinacantecos have added 17 new cargos to their yearly round, created a number of new voluntary organizations, and established waiting lists to accommodate the excess of men ready and willing to be sponsors.

Structurally, the fiesta system of Zinacantán is hierarchical, its posts being organized into four levels. Men begin their ceremonial careers serving a first-level post. Some of them proceed through complete careers by discharging one post on each level. Sponsorship is costly in time, money, and food, though some cargos are much more expensive than others.

Cancian discusses two ways in which men are induced to shoulder the burden of cargo service. The system is basically coercive, or was until recently; up to a few years ago the community elders had the unqualified power to jail anyone they could not persuade or shame into doing his religious duty. Given the level of commitment that has existed in Zinacantán, this apparently was not often necessary, but when it was, there was no one to stand in the elders' way. Through voluntary service, on the other hand, men could earn the positive rewards of esteem and social standing in the community. Cancian shows that any adult's standing in the eyes of his peers is closely determined by his ritual service. This leads Cancian to interpret cargo sponsorship primarily in terms of prestige striving. Zinacantecos, he implies, rather uniformly prize the prestige of sponsorship, so much so that there is little deviance from ceremonial norms, little reluctance to participate, and little need for coercive sanctions.

Questions of motivation are important to Cancian's analysis but are not his primary interest. He demonstrates that men do indeed earn prestige in ritual service, but, instead of asking why prestige should be attached to such behavior, he asks what the effects of the behavior are on community social structure. In developing his explanation of ritual equilibrium, he outlines what appears to be an excellent case of how a peasant community armors itself with its own institutions.

His central idea is that the cargo system serves as a kind of social "insulation" that operates from the inside to preserve the community's distinctively Indian integration. As long as there is full participation in the cargo system, Cancian asserts, commitment to native symbols, kin patterns, and general way of life will be continually reaffirmed; the incidence of envy and witchcraft will be reduced; and there will be a minimum of "potentially disruptive innovation and competition" (1965:134-35). The cargo institution is depicted as a superorganic entity that enmeshes men psychologically and socially in their Indian world and, more significantly, consumes the surplus wealth they might otherwise invest in cultural change. Because of festive giving, the argument goes, capital accumulation

> that might be used for non-Indian types of investment is severely limited. In addition, of course, this enforced expenditure of wealth prohibits many excursions into the Ladino world of consumption that Zinacantecos might otherwise make (1965:136).

The cargo system is thus offered as the key to community integration and to the preservation of social boundaries between local Indians and regional Ladinos. In sum, "The cargo system is crucial to the continued existence of

Zinacantan as an Indian community, a community separate and distinct from its Ladino environment'' (1965:133).

The organismic quality of this idea of homeostatic rituals is clearly expressed but by no means novel in Cancian's work. There is a tradition in Mesoamerican studies of portraying the fiesta system as an important basis and cause of Indian cultural stability; Cancian is the latest, most sophisticated proponent of this tradition. But there is one unique feature that distinguishes his interpretation from earlier ones. This is the specific relationship he sees between ritual participation and community integration. Prior to his study, the fiesta system was thought to insulate the Indian community through economic leveling. Ritual spending was held to cut down the wealth of richer Indians, keeping them from becoming entrepreneurs. The community was in this way economically "leveled"; everyone shared more fully in its poverty, and no one could invest in social mobility or other divisive activities.

In reality, however, the fiesta system has virtually no effect on the distribution of community income, since it occasions episodes of heightened consumption, not income redistribution. Cancian's statistics consequently show that Zinacantán is highly stratified, despite its demanding ceremonial system, and, in fact, that the most impressive sponsors tend to come from lineages with a history of impressive sponsorship (1965:109-16). Because sponsorship does not level wealth, leveling cannot be the mechanism of community integration. In its place, Cancian advances an alternative "stratifying" hypothesis, which holds that since rituals reward the rich with greater prestige, they promote solidarity by sanctifying and rendering socially legitimate these already existing inequalities.

The stratifying hypothesis is a revised view, but it reverses the picture without damaging the standard organismic interpretation. Whereas it was once argued that equality integrated the community, it is now argued that "legitimate" inequality does so. Cohesion springs from a new mechanism, but the mechanism is still an internal element of community structure.

Integration through stratification is the central idea of what Cancian calls his "synchronic" analysis of the stabilizing role of the cargo system in Zinacanteco social structure. He then turns to his "diachronic" analysis, where he discusses the disequilibrium he feels will strike the cargo system and the community in the near future. If the cargos insulate the community against the outside world, the implication is that Zinacantecos cannot engage in social mobility, entrepreneurship, or other kinds of new behavior so long as the ritual system is operating in normal fashion. This integrating and segregating mechanism must be somehow switched off before people can take matters into their own hands and begin to innovate. Openings for innovative behavior will develop, Cancian thinks, as rates of population growth and wealth accumulation in Zinacantán become too steep for the cargo system to handle.

His predictions for the future are as follows: population growth (which he sees as the primary threat to ritual integration), augmented by growing surpluses of wealth, is expanding the number of men who want cargo offices. This creates a new demand that, in the long run, the system cannot meet. Full participation and the integration it produces will consequently be threatened as people who are excluded from ritual sponsorship look to the outside world to satisfy their prestige ambitions. The creation of waiting lists and new cargos tends to counteract this imbalance, but is at best a stop-gap solution to the problem. The cargo system

> is not providing enough positions for the growing population. For more than a decade the waiting lists have absorbed the surplus, but it is improbable that men will be satisfied with a situation in which they must wait more than twenty years for a cargo. In a few years the waiting lists as well as the cargo system will be full to capacity, and there will be no way to handle the demands of men seeking to establish their positions in the community (1965:186).

Furthermore,

> Insofar as there is less than full participation, the integration of the society would be weakened, for the part of the population that would be left out of the cargo system would not be committed to the community. . . . Presumably, those who would not participate would look elsewhere for sources of prestige, and would further weaken community integration by introducing alternative prestige symbols, which would compete with the cargo system's (1965:170).

According to Cancian's argument, cultural change will thus begin only after community population has become too large for the ritual insulation to contain. Being "left out of the cargo system," some people will lose their sense of Indian commitment and in their frustration will disrupt Indian integration by turning to Ladino prestige symbols. Wealth accumulation will then reinforce this population effect, for Zinacanteco incomes are rising too fast for the cargo system to burn off their reserves. With surplus wealth on their hands, the Indians' frustrations will be intensified, and they will have the funds to experiment with new activities:

> insofar as the traditionally defined cargo system does not consume the
> increasing wealth of the community, this wealth is available to indi-
> viduals for other uses—uses that may very well be found in the Ladino
> rather than the Indian way of living (1965:141).

With this diachronic analysis, Cancian rounds out his functional interpretation of the fiesta system in Zinacantán, the important points of which are:

1. Men sponsor cargos in order to earn prestige in the community.
2. In so doing, they enhance both the cohesion of the group and its
   separation from dominant Mexican society; they create an insulating
   ethnic boundary.
3. Cohesion is strengthened through the stratifying effects of the system.
4. Separation is preserved through the system's channeling of surplus
   wealth away from Ladino investments.
5. Acculturation is inevitable, but will begin only after population
   becomes too large and wealth too abundant for the ritual insulation to
   contain.

Logic of the Functional Explanation

One of the most amazing aspects of functional theory is how resistant, how
absolutely impervious, it is to criticism. "The Dismal Science of
Functionalism," Gregg's and William's major logical and ethical critique,
appeared as early as 1948. Leach attacked functionalism from the field in
Political Systems of Highland Burma (1965) for its inability to handle real,
dynamic social situations. In 1959 Hempel found it full of tautologies, and
having heuristic value only. Homans's presidential address to the American
Sociological Association was a frontal assault which concluded that
functionalism has "never produced a functional theory that was in fact an
explanation" (1964:818). Yet despite these weighty attacks, functionalist
studies continue to appear, most of them leaving the impression that
functionalism is as acceptable as the law of gravity.

Cancian's analysis of the cargo system is in the classical tradition of
Radcliffe-Brown. When Cancian looks at cargo rituals as an element of
community structure and asks what these things are doing to preserve the
whole, he is following in the footsteps of Radcliffe-Brown, who asked the
same question of Andamanse ritual over a half-century ago (1922). Both men

seem to see society as an organism that employs its rituals as a mollusk employs calcium, to blindly evolve a self-preserving shell.

Functionalists reach such conclusions by abstracting a pattern from real events, reifying the pattern as an "institution," then playing it back against behavior as an explanation for stability. Cancian's functionalism, however, must go even a step further than Radcliffe-Brown's, since social stability is a more complex matter in peasant societies. The Andamanse were a relatively isolated island group, so Radcliffe-Brown could explain their social cohesion as the result of shared sentiments created by their religious behaviors. Cancian must assert this and more, because Zinacantán is not geographically isolated from cultural alternatives. Since Zinacantecos can potentially become Ladinos, his system stabilizer must not only provide continuity of sentiment but inhibit acculturation as well. This accounts for his arguments that the cargo system precludes innovative spending, and that the cargos will disappear not as part of a broader pattern of social and cultural change but as a necessary precondition to that change.

The fundamental problem with this approach is that holding up a particular institution as the cause of social action emphasizes the form of behavior rather than the conditions that shape it. Murdock has shown the error in such arguments—arguments which he finds so common in our discipline that he refers to them as "anthropology's mythology" (1971). In Murdock's view, only two phenomena can be legitimately employed in explaining complex human behavior. One is the unique human capacities to sense, learn, remember, and so on. These capacities are the "mechanisms" of behavior, which are explanatory in conjunction with the second set of phenomena, the "conditions" of behavior. These conditions consist of the extraordinarily varied environments in which human actors play out their lives. From this perspective, "culture" and "social structure," the major concepts of anthropology, define the results of the interplay between human beings and the conditions of their existence, but they explain nothing. The concepts of culture and social structure, Murdock says, are useful metaphorically and organizationally, but under no circumstances "is it safe or proper to employ them as operating or explanatory principles." They are at best "the results of the interaction of individual human beings; as reified abstractions they can never be causes or operant factors in behavior" (1971:22).

Studies of the fiesta system substantiate Murdock's point. When one assumes that the peasant community is a superorganic, self-stabilizing system that manufactures its own cultural insulation, problems of reification, of tautology, and of empirical omissions immediately are visible. To begin with, an abstraction is held to control the actions of real people coping with real environments. The argument that the fiesta institution is community insulation says, in essence, that what people tend to be doing keeps them from doing anything else. The functionalist position that consumption of wealth in the ritual system "impedes" capitalist investment and "prohibits" Ladino-style consumption, attributes causality to an abstraction rather than to the social and economic reality in which peasants allocate their resources. When people spend their surpluses religiously rather than capitalistically, this is the result of a choice, not the cause of a choice. The institution, in other words, is there because of the spending pattern, not vice versa. Holding up "prestige-striving" as the motivation behind this kind of expenditure is no help, because prestige is linked to Ladino as well as Indian forms of spending, so we are still left wondering why Indians prefer to achieve it in the way that they do.

Thus a further effect of the insulation hypothesis is that it relegates to an unanalyzed residue the motivation behind ritual giving, and we never learn why the Indians exhibit the behavior that allegedly does such wonderful things for their social system. Answering this question would require analysis of how outsiders bar Indians from alternative social and economic opportunities, why they do so, how Indians respond to this treatment, what their economic and social resources are, how they reward one another for ritual giving, and why these rewards are effective. These questions are not asked and need not be asked so long as a reified abstraction is assumed to control human behavior.

Students of the fiesta system have been fixated on this kind of interpretation for years. Convinced that their abstractions are as explanatory as they are literary and elegant, they commonly talk as if communities really do catch people up and insulate them in "institutions," or shield them under the "weight of tradition." Almost all interpretations of the fiesta system stress this organismic, self-stabilizing theme. Major commentators such as Wolf, Nash, and Tax have espoused it, though they prefer the leveling to the stratifying variant. Nash says that:

> by using income and resources of individuals and of the community, the hierarchy keeps any one family from accumulating very much cash or property. . . . The rich, in local terms, cannot use their wealth for personal aggrandizement nor can they comfortably build houses which are patently superior to the average dwelling (1958:69).

Wolf says the same thing in different terminology:

> Like the thermostat activated by an increase in heat to shut off the furnace, expenditure in religious worship returns the distribution of wealth that might upset the existing equilibrium. In engineering parlance, it acts as a feedback, returning a system that is beginning to oscillate to its original course (1959:216).

Reina reiterates the theme endlessly in his study of Chinautla, where the "law of the saints"—his reified cause of community stability—"holds the community together and protects its culture" (1966:viii). Even Cancian, whose data demonstrate beyond doubt that the economically leveled peasant community is anthropological fiction, cannot resist bestowing on his new-found stratification the same integrating power previously attributed to the homogeneity he disproves.

From reified beginnings, functionalists proceed to tautological conclusions in their attempts to relate ceremonial giving to community integration. The proponents of stratification or of leveling have not verified that religious conservatism is the key to Indian cultural continuity—all that this shift demonstrates is that as long as community behavior is stable, this stability can be "functionally" related to rituals, whatever their effects on wealth distribution may be.

The tautology here lies in the questionable segregation of the fiesta system from community integration. The fiesta system does not cause integration, it *is* integration; ritual giving is more an indication of community cohesion than its creator. Demonstrating causality would require a comparative study, which the functionalists have yet to do. If they could show in a series of communities that only those with full-participation fiesta systems are highly Indian in all other ways, then they would have the beginnings of a case. But so far no one has made such a study, and if they did I doubt the relationship would be discovered (see De Walt 1975:97). There are many well-integrated Indian communities in Latin America, but Zinacantán is the only one described with a full-participation fiesta system, so integration can apparently spring from other sources. Besides, the case of San Miguel Ixtahuacán will show that so long as Indian communities are hemmed in by outside economic power they can preserve a large measure of their Indian culture and identity even while experiencing drastic changes in ceremonial life.

The overblown role attributed to the ritual institution stands out in starkest detail when functionalists are faced with explaining change in their self-stabilized communities. They have removed from the picture two factors essential to explaining change. The first of these is the potential that people display to act outside of their institutions, to consciously behave in ways that run counter to the traditional grain. The other and more important factor is the power of a changing environment to select, reinforce, extend, and expand these contrary behaviors. People emerge in the functional analyses as such bland, uniform, automatic creatures, as "oversocialized men," prodded here and there by their all-powerful institutions, who have few apparent capabilities other than the desire to be proper. As for the environment, once it is removed from the picture, it cannot be casually reintroduced for purposes of explaining change.

Because of these omissions, Cancian, in his diachronic analysis, seems a prisoner of the logic of his synchronic analysis. If ceremonial insulation keeps the community stable, men are not free to innovate (regardless of their resources, capabilities, or what may be happening in their environment) until they accidentally break this insulation down with the weight of their numbers and wealth. Only then, having unwittingly weakened the unintended armor, are those "left out of the cargo system" free and inspired to innovate. Having invested so much power in his reified stabilizer, the functionalist is compelled by his logic to find a weakness in it, an Achillean vulnerability to adventitious forces such as population growth, in order to explain change.

Earlier interpretations of the fiesta system follow much the same tack, though they are often less extreme than Cancian's. Adams, for example, clearly invokes the environment when he describes how post-Revolution political action affected village culture in Guatemala, but he thinks that the direct effect of this action was to strip away the "insulation" of the civil-religious hierarchy, thereby reducing the "Indian's resistance to culture change" and opening the way for further alterations (1957:48). In his famous article on closed corporate communities, Wolf describes at length the exploitative environments these communities faced in Mesoamerica and Java, yet he makes such a strong case for the fiesta system as an unconscious defensive response that to explain why these communities change he must fall back on the argument that, somehow, in the long run, "even the most efficient prestige economy cannot be counted on to dispose of all surplus wealth in the community." Due to this mysterious inadequacy, pools of surplus wealth accumulate in the closed communities, disrupt traditional integration, and provoke change (1967:242).

Cancian, too, brings in the environment in a tangential way, especially in his concluding speculations about the future of Zinacantán, but like Adams he feels that the environment becomes relevant only after the cargo system has lost its grip on human behavior. Zinacantán, he says, "is becoming ever more open to innovation as its insulation disappears. What takes place will depend in large part on what alternatives the environment offers" (1965:192).

Such statements portray the institution as the active agent and the environment as a vague, neutral place that cannot tempt men from their Indian duty as long as their religion is strong and that graciously *will* offer them alternatives as soon as their religion disintegrates. But is this really the case? Evidence from Guatemala and other investigations from Chiapas indicate that it is not. We shall see that in western Guatemala the strength of communal ritual institutions is related to the complex of geographic, demographic, economic, and political conditions under which people allocate their labor and other material resources. If this explanation has any validity, it should be possible to apply it to the case of Chiapas.

The two important questions are as follows. Are the outside conditions that Zinacantecos face really as passive as the functionalist interpretation implies, or has Zinacantán been frozen in its Indianness by external forces apart from the cargo system? What kinds of change is the community experiencing, and why is this change occurring? These questions are the basis of the next chapter.

FOUR

Another Look at Zinacantán

In their fascination with internal dynamics, the functionalists have missed the key to both community integration and the ritual organization of Zinacantán. Integration, ritual organization, and the changes now taking place in Zinacantán must be understood in the context of regional economic history.

Social Class in Chiapas

A number of writers have contributed to our understanding of the class structure of Chiapas. These investigators all make the same important points: power and wealth in regional society are sharply concentrated in the Ladino upper classes, lowland cash agriculture is the dominant form of production, virtually all rural people (whether Indian or Ladino) are caught in a labor-intensive economic trap, and rates of socioeconomic mobility are low. They also indicate that there is nothing new in this situation. For more than four centuries outside sources of power have conspired to benefit Ladino commercial interests at the expense of the campesinos. From this perspective cargo participation seems more a response to imposed limitations than a wellspring of community cohesion.

"One of the main concerns of Spanish colonizers in the New World," writes Murdo MacLeod, "was to find and control large agricultural populations" (1973:46). The conquerors of Middle America immediately put together an economic structure to accomplish this end. By 1540, scant decades after the Conquest, the Pacific zone of Chiapas, the Soconusco, became one of the area's major agricultural regions, as it continues to be to this day. The division between coastal cash agriculture and highlands subsistence agriculture had also evolved by this time, and the first labor intensive export crop (cacao) was under development (MacLeod 1973:44-48). By the 1540s highland Indians were involved in lowland plantation labor. By 1570 so many "foreign" Indians from Chiapas, Verapaz, and Quezaltenango were residing in Soconusco that a special judge had to be appointed to handle their cases (MacLeod 1973:70-79).

Demands on Indian labor continued through the indigo period, but they became much heavier with the post-Independence expansion of cash agriculture. During this period national governments promoted cash agriculture throughout the republic by selling land at cheap prices, encouraging foreign investment, and by breaking down "backward" institutions, especially the communal landholdings of the Church and the Indian communities. These developments magnified the basic class division in regional society, by strengthening the distinction between the elite, which controlled regional politics, labor, and increasing amounts of land, and the mass of agricultural laborers and subsistence farmers.

The effects of post-Independence changes on Chiapas and its Tzotzil Indians have recently been outlined by Wasserstrom (1976), who demonstrates that over the last 150 years cash agriculture in Chiapas has experienced an almost continuous period of expansion and capitalist integration. Utilization of Indian labor and usurpation of Indian land has been equally continuous during this growth episode. Soon after Independence, Ladino cattle ranches began to expand down the Grijalva basin, with the aid of Zinacanteco laborers and sharecroppers who were searching for alternatives to farming in the crowded highlands. The general expansion of commercial farming was promoted at this time by the state government, which was in great need of revenues, to such a degree that seizures of Indian lands ultimately provoked an uprising by Chamula Indians in 1869. In the later 1800s these processes were further accelerated by the vigorous expansion of coffee plantations in the Sierra Madre. Desperate for labor, plantation owners began contracting workers from among highland Indians, who they controlled with a vicious system of debt peonage. Oppression of Indian labor during this episode was pitiless (Pozas 1952). The explosive development of coffee farming attracted European and American capital, and utilized 10,000 workers each year.

Wasserstrom's reconstruction of the development of capitalist-export agriculture during the century preceding the Mexican Revolution is corroborated by Favre (1973:50-68). Favre shows that the number of latifundios in Chiapas grew steadily from 310 in 1837 to 950 in 1889, and that their value more than quadrupled during that same period. This epoch also witnessed the passage of political leadership into the hands of liberal and nationalist lowland entrepreneurs, a shift symbolized by the transfer of the regional capital in 1892 from the old colonial city of San Cristóbal to the lowland center of Tuxtla Gutiérrez. The roots of Chiapas society, in Favre's view, are to be found in this struggle over land, and in the Ladinos' ever-expanding control of the hot, rich lowlands. Dominating the tropical lowlands, he argues, allowed Ladinos to commercialize their operations and to amortize investments in a way that was well beyond the reach of Indian subsistence farmers. This in turn gave Ladinos control of Indian labor, and on top of this agrarian power they also developed influence over vital connections in the regional markets for food, handicraft goods, and industrial commodities. The Indians, thus, presently occupy a status even worse than that of a wage-earning proletariat. The Indian, according to Favre, "is not exploited solely as a worker, but also as a producer and consumer" (1973:100).

The energetic expansion of coffee and cattle in the lowlands ultimately made Chiapas into a major export region in which the profitable production of cash crops was based on cheap highlands labor. Export agriculture developed even further when World War II expanded the market for beef, and when the Pan American Highway linking the highlands with the Grijalva valley was completed in 1947. This continuing elaboration of Chiapas agribusiness, according to Wasserstrom, has further amplified the connections between the subsistence and cash sectors by establishing lowland tenant farming as an important adjunct to highlands subsistence (see also Cancian 1972). To maintain corn productivity, Grijalva ranchers began renting land to Indians, who continued to seek alternatives to their overworked highlands. The practice of tenant farming, which by 1975 had carried Zinacanteco *milperos* down the Grijalva to the Guatemalan border, presently provides a number of significant benefits to the ranchers. Indian renters provide ranchers with cheap farm labor, as well as with a proportion of their harvests that has recently risen as high as 44 percent. The corn that the ranchers realize as rent is often sold for profit. Renters also clear land for *milpas* that the ranchers ultimately reclaim for pasture.

This eagerness on the part of Zinacantecos to rent land exposes the Mexican land reform movement's failure to improve conditions in the highlands, and reveals that its true intent was agricultural development, not agrarian justice. As the reform movement gathered speed during the Cárdenas administration it spawned a complex of agencies and programs that incorporated Indian leaders who were used as local political instruments. In this way, according to Wasserstrom (n.d.:223-29) the various relations between the subsistence and cash sectors came to be reinforced by a centralized Ladino and Indian bureaucracy that had as its primary interest not balancing the distribution of land, but the continued development of lowland agriculture. Such a program required that Indian land agitation not discourage private enterprise, and that the Indians be induced to cooperate with the continued expansion of ranching. The land reform agencies were apparently successful at their task. Some land was redistributed to highland Indians, but not in sufficient quantity to alter the basic agrarian structure of the region. Latifundios in the Grijalva valley passed through the Cárdenas period almost wholly intact, and after a brief decline stockraising began to grow spectacularly, expanding fourfold between 1955 and 1960. The fragmentation and control of the Indians through incorporation of certain leaders into the controlling apparatus, furthermore, became so pervasive that it now extends all the way down to the rental of lowland plots. Most rentals are negotiated by Zinacanteco foremen, who monopolize relations with Ladino ranchers. These foremen in turn exploit their position by including Chamulas in their groups, to whom they allocate inferior and rocky plots. The land reform period clearly demonstrates that latter-day Ladinos have not forgotten the old Spanish techniques of divide-and-rule and indirect government through coopted Indian leadership.

This concentration of power in Ladino hands in conjunction with their urgent need for Indian labor to expand and run their farms is the basis of the strong class barriers in Chiapas society, barriers that have distinct ethnic correlates. Ethnic groups and classes do not coincide in Chiapas. As we have seen, many Indians cooperate with Ladino farmers and the state bureaucracy, while at the same time Chiapas has a large population of rural Ladino subsistence farmers and wage laborers whose economic position is no different from that of most Indians. Ethnicity and class, however, do overlap to an important degree, as Siverts (1969) shows in his analysis of contemporary social boundaries in the highlands. Siverts's central interest, similar to Cancian's, is to explain the persistence of distinct cultural "idioms" in the highlands, but he does this from the viewpoint of the interaction of ethnic groups rather than that of a community institution. The thrust of Siverts's analysis is that Ladinos dominate most political and economic assets, and so dominate the Indians. Ladinos run the schools, admitting few Indians to the secondary level, and they administer the labor market, thus playing a controlling role in regional trade. Ladinos also dominate the countryside politically through their legal and administrative apparatus, and substantiate their position with force. It is these structural boundaries in regional society, according to Siverts, that ultimately maintain the Indians as a distinct cultural community. The boundaries in this sense perserve the idioms; the idioms do not preserve the boundaries (see Margolies 1975 for a parallel analysis of another Mexican region).

Colby and van den Berghe paint a similar picture of contemporary Ladino domination. Ladinos, they say, commonly treat Indians in a contemptuous and condescending manner, cheat them on weights and prices, and have even been known to set aside diseased meat for Indian customers. So arrogant are these people that until recently they forbade Indians to ride horses and to walk on the sidewalks of San Cristóbal (1961:779, 781). The investigators describe the town itself as being "rigidly stratified, and its inhabitants strongly class-conscious." Townspeople conceive of themselves as divided into three classes, an upper class called *la crema* or *los blancos,* a middle class, and a low class of *gente humilde*. The low "humilde" class is made up of poor Ladinos and Indian migrants to the city (1961:772).

Elsewhere Colby and van den Berghe show that the majority of Ladinos have an unfavorable opinion of Indian customs and are increasingly opposed to Indian contact as it becomes more intimate and egalitarian. Ladinos will stand as godparents for Indian infants, but never choose Indians as godparents for their children, a typical pattern of co-parenthood which underlines and symbolizes social inequality. Indian women are regularly taken as concubines, but intermarriage is rare and strongly disapproved of. Ladinos generally think of themselves as superior to Indians and have a paternalistic view of ethnic relations. Indians see themselves simply as different from Ladinos, not as inferior to them. They view ethnic relations in terms of struggle and competition (van den Berghe and Colby 1961; van den Berghe and van den Berghe 1966; see also Vogt 1969:30-31).

Clearly, within the regional society the distribution of economic and social opportunity is strongly restricted and controlled by a powerful non-Indian group and its Indian allies, and this pattern has penetrated so deeply into the local culture that even highly symbolic institutions such as ritual kinship now underscore the lines of material inequality. No one can understand the stability of Indian culture by studying just the Indians while ignoring regional stratification and the advantages Ladinos earn from the ethnic status quo. These regional studies indicate that Zinacantán has been kept in its narrow Indian position by economically motivated Ladino domination, not by the cargo system.

This broader perspective explains why Zinacantán has been a cohesive Indian community and why Zinacanatecos have expressed this in such elaborate ceremonial ways. As long as it has been dominated by a powerful agrarian society, conditions favoring ritual giving in Zinacantán have been strong. Zinacantecos are part of a capitalist society, but they are *not* the capitalists and so are little involved in the metropolitan economy with its multiple uses for surpluses. Being excluded from cosmopolitan society, they are at the same time greatly involved with their little community and the evaluations of their neighbors. On the other hand, whatever the restrictions it suffers, Zinacantán has always been a prosperous place by peasant standards. We see operating in the history of Zinacantán a conjunction of forces: strong and confining economic pressures from above, in combination with an abundant subsistence economy. Zinacantán is clearly better off than San Miguel Ixtahuacán since it produces a large food surplus and has a significant cash income. But it has not yet broken through the barriers that isolate it from broad and effective participation in national life, as San Pedro Sacatepéquez has. From the perspective of their place in regional society and economy, it thus seems reasonable that many Zinacantecos should continue to play the cargo game, and to play it in high style. Why shouldn't they? They can afford it, and for them it's the only game in town.

The Future of the Cargo System

The role of the cargo system in the history of Chiapas is identical to its role everywhere: it is part of a superstructure of political control in that it provides the Indians with basic human satisfactions in a way that fractures their total population into insular community fragments that cannot easily threaten the state. By dividing and channeling the Indians' energies into local rather than national or regional class affairs, the fiesta system dilutes the numerical power of the Indians, making them more easily controlled by the Ladino minority. The cargo system in Zinacantán makes most sense when viewed as a kind of palliative for those on the bottom of an exploitative regional society. It provides Zinacantecos with the kind of psychic gratifications that the powerful classes can afford to let them have—in fact, cannot afford *not* to let them have—gratifications that help stabilize the regional social system without threatening the privileges of its elite. The system is a palliative for Zinacantecos because it lessens the pain of subordination while doing nothing to eliminate its causes. Because of the cargo system, the Zinacantecos' cultural alternative is not a pathological void but a positive adaptation rich in ego satisfactions. Its only drawback is that while it gratifies the local community it contributes nothing to Indian class solidarity.

Given these strong pressures, how will change come about in Zinacantán? The best indications we have of the future of this community and its fiesta system are found in Wasserstrom's (1974 and n.d.) descriptions of the ways Zinacantecos have modified their ritual life in recent decades. The picture Wasserstrom paints of Zinacantán is one of a diversified set of hamlets that are highly responsive to changes in the outside world, and that relate to each other in complex ways. Particularly interesting is his discussion of the construction of new chapels in six Zinacanteco hamlets, and the effect of these chapels on the community's central cargo structure. By placing recent ritual change in its larger historical and economic context, Wasserstrom demonstrates that the new hamlet festivals represent an attempt by some Zinacantecos to perpetuate their native identity, while at the same time relieving themselves of the expenses associated with traditional cargo participation. The new fiestas, in other words, represent a pulling away on the part of some hamlets from the conventional hierarchy, although these hamlets have not abandoned their commitment to the Indian lifestyle.

Cancian and Vogt also recognize the importance of the new hamlet fiestas, but their functionalist interpretations miss the true significance of these fiestas. Cancian (1965:162-73) sees the new chapels and associated fiestas as equilibrating innovations that serve, along with the waiting lists, to stave off the day when Zinacantán's population finally becomes too large to be accomodated by the hierarchy. Vogt (1969:271, see also Cancian 1965:viii) thinks the new fiestas might signal the coming segmentation of Zinacantán into a series of communities each with its own cargo system. These interpretations are so focused on internal balances and equilibrium that they neglect the impact of regional development on Zinacanteco social structure, which Wasserstrom's economic history so clearly reveals. According to Wasserstrom's reconstruction, the rapid expansion of cattle ranching in the Grijalva valley along with the opening of the Pan American Highway strongly favored certain Zinacanteco hamlets, where they promoted considerable economic growth. Zinacantán at present is an economically divided municipio, a fact that goes unrecognized in studies that deal with the community on holistic and institutional levels. The more prosperous hamlets are those scattered along Zinacantán's southwestern rim, overlooking the Grijalva, and near the Pan American Highway. These hamlets have so benefitted from regional development that some now surpass Zinacantán center in wealth and population.

Development began in these hamlets as Ladino ranches spread down the Grijalva valley. By the 1930s Zinacantecos were sharecropping on some 20 large lowland haciendas, clearing brush to plant milpas that would ultimately become pasture. Although it was a subsistence activity for some Zinacantecos, others, especially those with many sons, developed sharecropping into a commercial enterprise. These men became wealthy by investing their surpluses in mules, which they used to transport lowland corn harvests. The Pan American Highway, which runs through the municipio, provided these Zinacantecos with even more opportunities. The new highway system allowed many farmers to move their operations into distant virgin territory. Others began cultivating commercial crops such as flowers and fruit to sell in now-accessible lowland markets. Still other Zinacantecos purchased trucks; between 1957 and 1974 some 30 men purchased close to 40 vehicles. Consumerism also rose during this period, as more prosperous Zinacantecos began buying radios, clothing and other inexpensive industrial goods.

The most interesting thing about these economic developments is that they are strongly concentrated in just those hamlets where ritual modifications in the form of new chapels and hamlet fiestas have been instituted. Nabenchauk, for example, a hamlet founded in the mid-19th century, grew rapidly after 1930, and became so large and important after the opening of the Highway that it is now an *agencia municipal* (a semi-autonomous municipal corporation). In 1957 the people of Nabenchauk responded to their new-found prosperity by founding two cargos in their hamlet chapel, where they now discharge ceremonial obligations without the expense and loss of time required by traditional service in Zinacantán center. The people of Nabenchauk no longer live up to the norm of full participation. Fewer than half the men who serve hamlet cargos pursue further service in the traditional hierarchy, and fully a third of the men of Nabenchauk have accepted no ceremonial offices at all, either in the hamlet or in the center. Similar fiestas have been recently established in five other hamlets. Four of these hamlets have established chapel committees instead of cargos, and in so doing have directly rejected the concept of individual ritual sponsorship. These committees are cooperative, volunteer organizations that maintain hamlet chapels, and collect funds to finance hamlet fiestas.

Wasserstrom's information indicates that with the new infrastructure developments, especially the roads, Zinacantecos are no longer so completely sealed off from profitable economic activities. Changes in the environment, in

other words, are not only going to influence community life in Zinacantán—
they already have. Some hamlets have experienced significant development
and diversification over the last half-century or so, changes that have inspired
many of their residents to avoid the ritual burdens that give the cargo system
its name. As they responded to new outside opportunities, and as their
hamlets rose in population and stature, these men shifted their allegiance from
municipal to local saints and ceremonies. Their sense of Indianness and
attachment to native culture remains strong, however, because these new
enterprises have not mixed them into the urban Ladino environment. The new
ceremonies they established have thus allowed them to continue to celebrate
their ethnic and local solidarity, but to do so in a manner that *they* control. The
cargo system has not insulated Zinacanteco entrepreneurs from the outside
world. On the contrary, these entrepreneurs have modified the cargo system
in direct response to their new needs and possibilities.

Similar changes have been accumulating in the environment of Guatemalan Indian communities over the last century. They are strongly although not
exclusively associated with a growing capitalist impetus. The expansion of
plantation agriculture on the Pacific coast, in conjunction with Indian population growth in the highlands, has transformed much of the previously self-
sufficient highland population into a seasonal proletariat. On a much smaller
scale, a few Indian communities have themselves become capitalist, especially in the areas of transport, commerce, and small-scale manufacturing.
Political and social relations have also been altered in important ways, such
that no Indian village, however hidden in the rugged sierras, is the folkish
world-unto-itself that all villages were just a few decades ago.

The following chapters describe two Indian communities that exemplify
these trends. One is heavily proletarianized, the other rapidly modernizing.
The aim in both cases is to show how these new forms of national involvement have altered Indian ritual life.

FIVE

Highland San Marcos

San Marcos is one of the westernmost departments of the Republic of Guatemala. It borders on the departments of Huehuetenango to the north, Quezaltenango and Retalhuleu to the east, the Pacific Ocean to the south, and the Mexican state of Chiapas to the west. Geographically and ecologically the department is extremely diverse. It contains high volcanoes, intermontane valleys, a steep escarpment cut by fast-running rivers, and a torrid coastal plain. The highest mountain peak and the highest human community in all of Central America are found in the *tierra fria* of San Marcos. Its agricultural products range from sheep and potatoes in the upper elevations to cotton and bananas on the tropical Pacific coast.

In the highlands of this department the adjacent towns of San Marcos (Ladino) and San Pedro (Indian) constitute the only urban zone and serve as the administrative, educational, and commercial center for the entire highlands population.[1] The four principal roads, all of which were unpaved at the time of my study, branch out from this center: one leads into the interior mountains, two go down to the coast, and one goes out to the town of Quezaltenango, where it connects with the Pan American Highway. Outside this single urban center, population in the mountains is highly dispersed.

The department is divided ethnically and economically into two major regions, the highlands and the coast. In the former, Indians and Indian culture predominate—almost 75 percent of the highland population identifies itself as Indian. As a group, the Indians own most of the land, produce most of the food, and operate most of the commerce in the highlands. Ladinos, in contrast, fill the roles of administrators, educators, and professionals. They control the government and social services, which has given them great power. Although they are now being challenged by the emerging Indian bourgeoisie of San Pedro, Ladinos have always been at the top of the social order in San Marcos, despite being the minority group.

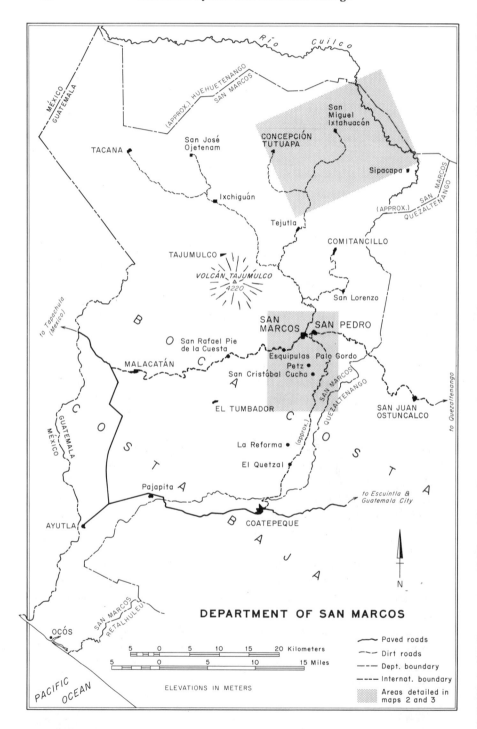

DEPARTMENT OF SAN MARCOS

	Paved roads
	Dirt roads
	Dept. boundary
	Internat. boundary
	Areas detailed in maps 2 and 3

5   0   5   10   15   20 Kilometers

5   0   5   10   15 Miles

ELEVATIONS IN METERS

Ladinos dominate on the coast as well, where they own most of the land in addition to their other prerogatives. Local people recognize two zones within the coastal region: the escarpment of the sierra, called the *boca costa,* which is devoted principally to coffee production, and the *costa baja,* the Pacific coast plain, a zone of cattle ranching, and commercial corn and cotton farming. In San Marcos and southeastward throughout the republic, these hot, rich areas are zones of commercial agriculture. The semitropical slopes and tropical plain of the Pacific coast contain the most productive agricultural land in the entire country. Many Indians live in these regions, but they own little land and form no independent communities. True Indian communities stop where the zone of commercial coffee-growing begins.

The highlands and the coast have long been integrated into a regional economy through goods and labor markets. Even before the introduction of trucks there was trade in subsistence goods between these regions. This earlier trade was facilitated primarily by peasant Indian *comerciantes* (merchants) of San Pedro Sacatepéquez and San Cristóbal Cucho, who, living on the edge of the escarpment, had access to both the coast and the interior mountains. Trading was carried on through a network of *plaza* markets in the principal population centers. Because the interior and coastal markets convened on weekends, the comerciantes who worked each area met on Thursdays in the giant plaza of San Pedro to exchange goods. Historically, the San Pedro plaza was both a retail market serving a large surrounding area and a wholesale market in which Indian merchants purchased one another's wares.

The trade network that connected the mountain communities with the Pacific tropics was recapitulated on the interior edge of the Sierra Madre. As one proceeds northward through the mountains past the *municipio* (township) of Concepción Tutuapa, the land again drops steeply into the interior valley of the Rio Cuilco. This valley separates the Sierra Madre from the Altos Cuchumatanes of Huehuetenango and is a hot zone of citrus and coffee production, so similar in climate and agriculture to the Pacific coast that Indians refer to them both as *costa*. Here, once more, geographical diversity stimulated peasant trade, and men from Concepción Tutuapa and San Miguel Ixtahuacán made regular trips to the Cuilco lowlands, the villages of the Cuchumatanes, and the large markets in and around Quezaltenango. This trade does not seem to have been as highly elaborated or as intense, however, as that centering on San Pedro, probably because population in the interior mountains was more dispersed and sparser than on the Pacific edge of the sierra.

This trade system still operates today, with a few significant alterations. With new and improved roads, San Pedro has become even more important commercially; it is a major center of trucking, retailing, and textile production. The range of San Pedro's influence is also increasing, even in the mountains where roads to San Miguel, Concepción, and Tacaná have reduced the isolation of interior populations. New plazas are being established in mountain villages and old ones are growing, especially the Thursday market in Concepción Tutuapa, which is beginning to rival that of San Pedro in size.

The highlands and the coast are also linked by the demand for seasonal labor on the commercial farms of the coast. Ever since the establishment of the coffee industry in the latter half of the nineteenth century, large landholders have gone to great lengths to assure themselves an abundant supply of cheap Indian labor. Debt peonage was their first tactic, followed by the notorious vagrancy laws of the Ubico dictatorship. Such blatant labor coercion was abolished by the 1944 Revolution, only to be replaced by a form more subtle and natural but equally compulsory. Recent population growth in the highlands has been so rapid that many communities, especially in the interior mountains, no longer produce enough corn to carry them through the year. These communities now depend on coastal corn, which they purchase with wages earned on the coffee and cotton plantations. In San Marcos, Indians are no longer duped or coerced into plantation labor. They have been forced into it because they have outgrown their subsistence base.

Agrarian problems in highland San Marcos are confined primarily to the interior communities and point up the basic inequities in the regional economy. Although the interior communities both supply the labor that underwrites the prosperity of the coast and purchase much of the goods sold by the merchants of San Pedro, their contributions to the commercial sector are not equally returned. Proletarian Indians earn a subsistence wage with which they purchase subsistence goods. Their overall economic situation is degenerating. From an economic perspective, we can divide the highlands of San Marcos into two subregions: the highly proletarian and dependent interior, and the increasingly prosperous area centering on San Pedro and San Marcos.

The highlands are organized into a complex, plural society. Today five major cultural and economic groups can be identified. First, there are the urban Ladinos who live either in the town of San Marcos or scattered about the countryside, where they work as officials or rural schoolteachers. These people are literate participants in the national culture and society; they stand in striking contrast to a second group of poorer, more provincial Ladinos. The provincial Ladinos, or "half-way Ladinos" as one urbanite called them, are *campesino* farmers and craftsmen who live either as small minorities in the interior Indian municipios or in one of the several predominantly Ladino municipios of the area. These Ladinos are peasants rather than townsmen. Most of them are poorly educated, and their living standards and aspirations differ little from those of rural Indians.

Finally, the Indian sector of the regional society can be divided into three major groups: the few remaining independent peasants, the *gente civilizada* (acculturated Indians) now found in the town of San Pedro and in the hamlets on its outskirts, and the proletarianized Indians of the interior mountains who live by farming and yearly labor transhumance. The peasant group was originally much larger, being the basic class to which most Indians belonged before the elaboration of the agricultural labor market and the commercialization of San Pedro.

Contemporary regional society in the highlands is thus not a simple plural society of urban Ladinos and rural Indians. In highland San Marcos there are profound cultural and economic differences between progressive townsmen, who are both Indian and Ladino, and country folk, who are also of both ethnic groups. Furthermore, in the countryside, there is an important economic difference between communities of subsistence farmers, whether Indian or Ladino, and the Indian municipios of the interior mountains, where wage labor is a vital adjunct to subsistence farming.

The Township of San Miguel Ixtahuacán

Ixtahuacán is an insular community in many ways. Few of its residents have left the municipio to seek their fortunes in the outside world. Most are illiterate or semiliterate. Mam, the local Maya language, is still the language of preference, although most men and many women can converse in crude Spanish. All men are farmers, but few produce enough grain to see their families through the year. Living standards and aspirations are very low.

The municipio is composed of a *cabecera* (principal town) and 10 outlying *aldeas* (hamlets). The cabecera is the administrative and religious center of the township, the site of the *alcaldía* (township court house), the post office, the municipal treasury, and the major Catholic and Protestant churches. Two small plaza markets convene in the cabecera every week (the major weekly market is held in aldea El Triunfo because it is more accessible to traders from San Pedro and Tejutla). The community's primary connection with the outside world is a dirt road, which was recently extended from

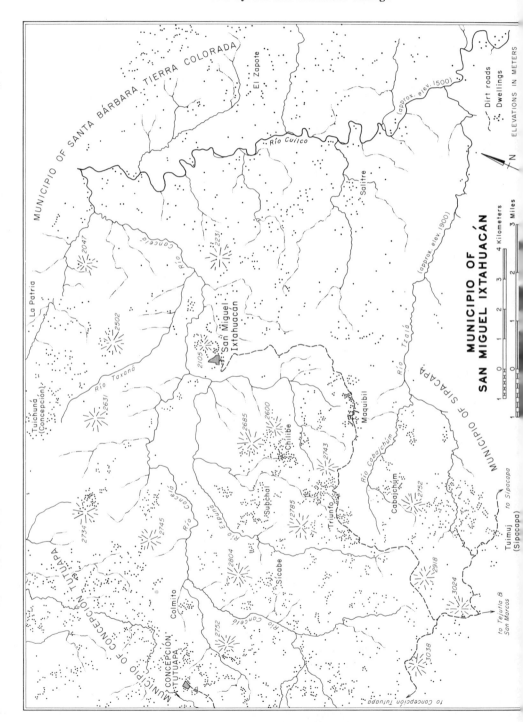

MUNICIPIO OF
SAN MIGUEL IXTAHUACÁN

Tejutla to the cabecera. There is now daily bus service between the cabecera and the San Marcos-San Pedro urban center, although a one-way trip still takes four hours.

Over 96 percent of the 9657 residents of the municipio were registered as Indians in the census of 1964. Most of the Indians live in aldeas scattered throughout the hills surrounding the cabecera. The cabecera is smaller than the aldeas, having only about 400 residents, and is populated mainly by Ladinos or Ladinoized people. The cabecera is in fact the only community in the township where people are dropping many of the overt symbols of Indian identity. There are virtually no Ladinos in the aldeas, other than school-teachers.

Local topography is highly diverse, and habitation ranges from a maximum altitude of around 8000 feet down to around 5000 feet in the valley of the Rio Cuilco near the eastern boundary of the township. Corn is the principal crop throughout this range. Wheat and sheep are important at higher altitudes; coffee, peaches, and citrus at lower ones. All farming is done by traditional hand methods, with hoes and machetes being the primary tools. The only important agricultural advance has been increasing use of chemical fertilizers and hybrid wheat seed by some farmers—although this has done little to reduce the community-wide deficit in basic grains. There is no significant cash-cropping in the muncipio.

Most commerce takes place in the plaza markets, especially the large one that meets every Saturday in aldea El Triunfo. Truckers and truck-borne comerciantes from San Pedro supply most of the goods to this market and carry away most of the profits. Miguelenses come either as peddlers (who are numerous but whose tiny operations are intensely competitive) or, more frequently, as consumers. The Triunfo market supplies most of the municipio's consumer needs: hardware, cloth, fertilizers, lowland produce such as rice and coffee, and most significantly, large quantitites of corn. It is also in this market that local people sell the few products they supply to the outside world. They buy, however, much more than they sell. The plaza markets in San Miguel are the means by which the community is provisioned, but they are of slight importance as a source of community income.

Miguelenses compensate for their grain deficits and trade imbalance with seasonal wage labor on coffee and cotton plantations. Each year the labor exodus beings in late August, when the first coffee is ripening, and continues through the end of the year and into January, when some men leave to cut cotton. Almost all families spend from one to three months in the coffee harvest, working mostly as family groups. Some families subsequently send a member or two to work in cotton as well. This labor market is highly organized. Each coffee plantation that uses Miguelense workers hires a number of local people as labor recruiters (called *habilitadores* or *agentes de finca*). Habilitadores contract workers, pay advances, and hire truckers from San Pedro to haul their gangs to the *fincas* (coffee plantations) when the beans are ripe. During the coffee harvest scarcely a day passes that a truck does not arrive to pick up its human cargo; at the peak of the season the municipio is a virtual ghost town.

Few Miguelenses have sufficient income to finance meaningful social mobility. Two men now own trucks, which they acquired by exploiting rare opportunities in administering finca labor, and both of these men have moved their families out of the municipio. Several of the more prosperous local families have managed to put some of their children through six to 12 years of school. The residents of the cabecera are Ladinoized to some extent, but this change has been confined primarily to their self-image. The grammar school in the cabecera is well equipped and well staffed, and the village ambiance is highly Ladino because of the public servants who reside there. Young cabecera Indians are consequently adopting Ladino clothing and denying knowledge of Mam, but their standard of living and material possibilities are no different from those of aldean campesinos.

My estimate is that economic mobility and Ladinoization have affected at most 4 percent of the municipal population. Members of this broadly defined ''mobile'' category are generally the neo-Ladinos of the cabecera, whose new ethnic orientation has not affected their occupation or incomes. In the aldeas there has been virtually no upward mobility of any kind. Aldean people are not emigrating at any significant rate, their subsistence economy has deteriorated, their social orientation is strictly local, and their self-image is unambiguously Indian. We are all campesinos here, they say, and *indígenas* (Indians).

The most important new element in community social structure is the religious change and elaboration that has been occurring since the late 1950s. Although San Miguel was previously a folk-Catholic community maintaining its own body of rituals and shamans, traditional beliefs have lost ground to recent missionary effort. Unconverted people are still in the majority, but the Catholic and Protestant presence is definitely growing. The municipio now has a full-time minister of each faith, chapels are being built and renovated in the aldeas, and converted Catholics have regained control of the massive old convent in the cabecera, previously an important folk-Catholic shrine. Conversion is the most important social movement in the contemporary community, and religious orthodoxy is becoming a major institutional link between this remote community and Guatemalan society.

A picture of life in San Miguel can best be developed by looking at a representative municipal citizen. Casimiro López is in his early thirties and is a short man with a farmer's muscular body. He lives in a one-room adobe house—a dirt-floored hut constantly in a clutter, being too small to hold even his few worldly goods. Casimiro sleeps on a wood-plank bed, and his wife cooks over an open fire in a sooty outbuilding. Casimiro supports his wife and three children by farming milpa and wheat, and by peddling in the municipal plazas. He is a hard worker who is proud of his ability to withstand the rigors of his occupation. In January, for example, when he is preparing his fields for planting, he leaves his house "when the roosters sing," in the cold morning, and does not return home until after nightfall. Often he tires himself before beginning work, for land is in short supply and some of his fields are over an hour's walk from his house. Casimiro's life is toilsome and insecure. He lives with the fear of crop failure, and even in the best years and despite all his efforts he does not produce enough corn to feed his family.

But Casimiro is more fortunate than many of his people, for his hut is only a 45-minute walk from the El Triunfo market, and he has managed to build a stock of merchandise worth about 35 quetzales (Q35; one quetzal equals one dollar). Weekly peddling allows him to make up his farm deficit, so he does not have to contract himself to the finca. His income gives him no savings, however, and he harbors no aspirations for himself or his children. His oldest son is now in third grade, which will be his last year of schooling. Further education would be meaningless and expensive, and Casimiro can use his son's help around the farm. Besides, his boy has yet to receive the practical instruction he will need as a highlands *milpero*. "He doesn't even know how to cut wood," Casimiro says.

The Town of San Pedro

"Welcome to the modern and progressive *pueblo* of San Pedro," the sign announces at the entrance to town, courtesy of a local tailor shop. San Pedro is a unique Indian community, a large, concentrated town of over 10,000 people with a dynamic, developing economy, an evolving class structure, and

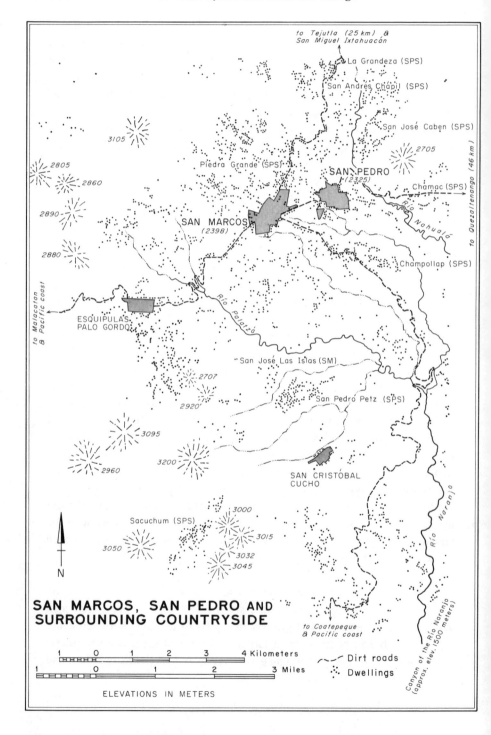

to Tejutla (25 km) &
San Miguel Ixtahuacán

La Grandeza (SPS)

San Andres Chapil (SPS)

San José Caben (SPS)

2705

3105

Piedra Grande (SPS)

SAN PEDRO
(2325)

Chamac (SPS)

Río Nahuala

to Quezaltenango (46 km)

2805

2860

SAN MARCOS
(2398)

2890

Champollap (SPS)

2880

to Malacatan
& Pacific coast

Río Palala

ESQUIPULAS,
PALO GORDO

San José Las Islas (SM)

2707

San Pedro Petz (SPS)

2920

3095

3200

2960

SAN CRISTÓBAL
CUCHO

3000

Río Naranjo

Sacuchum (SPS)

3015

3050

3032

3045

N

SAN MARCOS, SAN PEDRO AND
SURROUNDING COUNTRYSIDE

to Coatepeque
& Pacific coast

Canyon of the Río Naranjo
(approx. elev. 1500 meters)

1   0   1   2   3   4 Kilometers

1   0   1   2   3 Miles

Dirt roads

Dwellings

ELEVATIONS IN METERS

a modernizing culture. The principal difference between San Pedro and the community just introduced is that San Pedro has bridged many of the gaps that separate the traditional and modern sectors of Guatemalan society. While mobility in San Miguel Ixtahuacán is restricted to occasional cases of individual "passing," in San Pedro it has become an institutionalized process, a social movement affecting the entire group. Over about the last three decades this community has been in a phase of self-sustaining, accelerating development.

San Pedro is immediately adjacent to the town of San Marcos, which is the departmental capital and major Ladino community in the region. San Pedro and San Marcos actually form a single urban agglomeration that is ethnically and administratively divided into two towns. Together they are the focal point of the highlands of this department, and they are often referred to locally as "twin cities." For twins, however, they are curiously different and bellicose. San Marcos is a service town. It is the site of departmental government and of health, military, and police facilities. The four major secondary schools in the department are also located in San Marcos, as are most of the doctors and lawyers. Consistent with their occupations, Marquenses (as the residents of this town are called) like to think of themselves as the regional representatives of national, cosmopolitan culture.

While Marquenses have been concerned with regional administration and services, San Pedranos have been busy in commerce. San Pedro has traditionally been the commercial center of this sector of the highlands, but recently, especially since around 1950, San Pedranos have developed and elaborated their trade advantages by investing in new kinds of capital and selling into expanding markets. All the major stores in San Pedro's sizable shopping district are Indian-owned. The plaza market is still large on Thursdays and is growing on other days of the week. San Pedro textiles are now sold in tourist shops of Guatemala City and are exported internationally. Mules have been replaced to a large degree by diesel trucks. Even the haughty Marquenses must shop in San Pedro, which has become the home of an emergent regional commercial elite.

It is impossible to characterize San Pedro in terms of a "typical" resident, as I did for San Miguel. The town is too complex, containing a variety of social types. The major distinctions between San Pedranos lie along cultural and occupational lines. Culturally, the town is divided into people who have a modern orientation (the *civilizados*) and those who, because of less education and their traditional dress and mode of life, are still *naturales*.

Occupationally, the townspeople range from craftsmen and campesinos through peddlers and shopkeepers, large merchants, truckers, and textile dealers, up to white-collar workers such as teachers, accountants, and lawyers. There is considerable overlap between the cultural and economic categories. Some of the wealthiest men in town are semiliterate, *natural* truckers.

The recent economic evolution of San Pedro has carried this town into a market position distinct from that of San Miguel Ixtahuacán. Markets in which powerless and ethnically distinct groups sell unskilled labor to commercial farms are invariably exploitative. This is especially true in countries such as Guatemala, where farm labor is illiterate and has no effective organization or leadership. The commercial market in San Pedro, on the other hand, has provided the community with expanding, multiplying opportunities. It has created real and obvious changes in peoples' possibilities, changes that are more than just economic. Contemporary San Pedranos are not simply prosperous Indians. New wealth has provoked changes in language, in styles of dress, in educational and consumer aspirations, and in self-image.

People in this town often refer to themselves as *gente civilizada* and to their community as a "civilized" pueblo. In using these terms they recognize themselves as a special class that is neither traditionally Indian nor strictly Ladino. These changes appear most strongly in the educational aspirations of contemporary San Pedranos. People in San Miguel Ixtahuacán consider three years of formal schooling to be adequate for their children's needs; San Pedranos want much more. The town has already produced one doctor, a handful of lawyers, and several hundred teachers. Many young San Pedranos attend San Marcos secondary schools, and the community is continually upgrading its own school system. Educational opportunities have grown along with San Pedro's broader participation in the national economy and social life of Guatemala.

The common use of terms such as "gente civilizada" indicates that changes in self-image and social character have also accompanied economic development. Wealth and knowledge are power, and San Pedranos are infused with a new sense of power. Their relations with San Marcos are intensely competitive, and as a group they feel increasingly competent to face the outside world on its own terms.

Petz and Cucho

The area around San Pedro can be thought of in terms of a folk-urban continuum, in which the remote villages of San Pedro Petz and San Cristóbal

Cucho form one pole, and San Pedro itsef the other (map 3). Petz is a hamlet of Indian campesinos that is part of the township of San Pedro Sacatepéquez (SPS). Cucho, a small town of Indians and Ladinos, is Petz's close neighbor, and is the cabecera of a separate municipio. These two communities are equally isolated from the twin cities. It is only four kilometers as the crow flies from Petz to San Pedro, but the trail is so steep and tortuous that the walk takes three exhausting hours. No road enters Petz; it will be years before one is cut through the deep ravines that isolate it from the outside world. Cucho is connected to the San Marcos-Coatepeque road but sees little commercial traffic and has no bus service.

The two communities provide an interesting contrast with San Pedro and San Miguel Ixtahuacán, being a kind of intermediate type, neither as progressive as the former nor as dependent as the latter. Although the people of Petz and Cucho are marginally involved in market activities, their economy is subsistence oriented and is productive enough to supply most of their food. As a consequence, relatively few of these people do wage labor outside their villages. Both communities have grammar schools, but few children study beyond the third grade, which shows how provincial and localized life is in these isolated spots. Many men are peddlers who supply the fincas of the adjacent coast with highland products, but this outside exposure has done nothing to modernize their lives. Providing for most of their own needs, and separated from the broader culture and society of the highlands, these villages can be best classified as an independent "peasant" type.

Rafael Fuentes of Petz is a good example of this peasant adaptation. Like most rural families, Rafael's is large: a wife, three sons, and two daughters. He and his wife learned Mam as children but now speak Spanish exclusively, as do their children. This is the common pattern in Petz and Cucho. Older people occasionally lapse into Mam, but Spanish is now the household language. Despite loss of the native language, Rafael's family still consider themselves Indian, and all of the women wear Indian costume.

Rafael is barely literate, his wife is illiterate. Their children have studied three years in the aldean school. His younger daughter, still in school, is a promising student, but Rafael doubts that he will allow her to continue studies. He sees no point to it, the expenses would increase as she went on to secondary school in San Pedro, and he harbors vague fears for her safety in the outside world. His attitude follows Casimiro's. Having little contact with cosmopolitan society, formal education beyond basic literacy is of small value to them.

Rafael spends most of his time in the village, cultivating corn and wheat. He also keeps a mule, several pigs, and two cows. On Thursdays he goes to San Pedro with his wife, for market. Previously this trip was part of Rafael's peddling business, but now they attend market only to buy spices and other specialties for the household. Rafael was a peddler as a young man, trekking down to the fincas of municipio El Quetzal every week to sell cheeses, sausages, and vegetables grown in the highlands. Over the years he saved enough to buy a small plot of coffee on the coast, and soon gave up peddling. Now he leaves the village even less frequently, since his tiny coffee orchard needs only periodic maintenance.

Although Rafael must work long and hard, his house is ample, his family is well clothed, and his fields and livestock are sufficient to provide his basic needs. He is developing a few consumer aspirations—he owns a radio and is considering flooring his house with concrete, as a few of his neighbors have recently done—but these desires are minimal and completely within his means. He enjoys a general well-being, however low his level of consumption. His means and standard of living are fairly representative of the populations of Petz and Cucho. There are a few Indians in Cucho whose holdings are much larger than Rafael's, and there are also some people in both villages who are noticeably poorer. But generally, the people of these villages share Rafael's stable, peasant way of life.

The continuation of this peasant orientation in Petz and Cucho is largely a result of the villages' geographical location. They are too removed from San Pedro to be strongly affected by the town's modernization. (In this regard they contrast sharply with aldeas such as Chamac, San José Caben, and Champollop. These latter villages, located on the very outskirts of the twin cities, within easy walking distance of schools, shops, and urban jobs, are showing definite tendencies toward modernization. They thus occupy a spot on the municipio continuum intermediate between the remote folk-like villages of Petz and Cucho and the central, progressive town of San Pedro.) Their location has also allowed Petz and Cucho to avoid the extreme dependence on plantation labor that San Miguel Ixtahuacán has suffered. San Miguel's present economic predicament is related to population expansion against fixed agricultural resources. Although rapid population growth is common to all highland communities, its effects vary from place to place. In San Pedro, for example, recent economic development has far outstripped population growth, so people are generally better off despite their increased numbers.

San Miguel Ixtahuacán, in contrast, is highly vulnerable to population pressure since in the interior mountains agricultural resorces are poor, and nonagricultural opportunities other than finca labor are virtually nonexistent.

Petz and Cucho are also agrarian communities, but they have the advantage of being situated on the very edge of the Sierra Madre, where the mountains plunge down to the Pacific Coast plain. Although they live at over 7000 feet, people from Petz and Cucho can walk to the coastal zones in a few hours, a feasible journey for a peddler or a farmer in search of land. As their population has grown in recent years, these people have stepped up exploitation of coastal opportunities. Access to this rich and distinct environment has allowed them to compensate for their population growth by extending traditional productive activities over a larger territory.

The basic comparisons in the chapters that follow will be between San Miguel Ixtahuacán and the town of San Pedro, to demonstrate how the fiesta system has responded to economic dependence in the first case and economic development in the second. Petz and Cucho provide a useful counterpoint to these primary cases. Being less affected by recent changes, they are contemporary examples of the earlier conditions that once were the foundation of ritual giving throughout the highlands municipios.

Notes

[1]Naming of various social units is very complex. San Marcos is the name of a town that is the administrative center of a township and of a department, both of which are also called San Marcos. San Pedro is the cabecera of a township whose full name is San Pedro Sacatepéquez. This township also contains a hamlet called San Pedro Petz. From here on I shall use San Marcos and San Pedro to refer to the respective towns only. When discussing the larger units that carry this name I will so specify.

SIX

The Ritual Background

The communities we have been discussing are inhabited by Indians of the Mam linguistic group. All of them previously maintained syncretic systems of belief and ritual, a set of locally venerated icons, and a contingent of shamanistic spiritual leaders. Participation in orthodox-Catholic ritual and acceptance of Catholic doctrine were minimal and selective, and in each community a set of sponsored ceremonies was the focal point of public religious activity. In recent years, expenditures for these ceremonies have ranged from about Q40 for a small aldean festivity in San Miguel Ixtahuacán to over Q400 for the *fiesta patronal* in San Pedro, plus three days to three weeks of ceremonial labor (see Table 1).

Petz and Cucho

People of the outlying community of Petz celebrate four fiestas a year—or sometimes three, since the Festival of the Virgen de Dolores is losing its popularity. Their other festivals, for San Pedro (the patron saint of the aldea), for Santiago, and for El Señor Sepultado, are still supported without fail. Each is sponsored by a single individual. To serve San Pedro or Santiago is expensive. One hundred quetzals for festival goods and services is a customary minimum expenditure, plus the time to prepare the celebration and to attend to the flowers at the saint's altar throughout the year. The ritual of El Señor Sepultado is a Holy Week rite, a *duelo* or wake for the dead Christ. The celebration is subdued and sorrowful, lacking the fireworks, dancing, and secular music that enliven other feast days, and is therefore less costly to the mayordomo.

   The community still observes the Maya custom of public service, but allows individuals some freedom in choosing their public careers. Two

TABLE I

Cofradía Expenditures: Labor and Wealth Consumed in Ritual Sponsorship, Communities of Highland San Marcos

Municipio & Community	Fiesta	Date	Man-Days Labor per Sponsor	Food, Drink, Entertainment	Ritual Goods/ Services	Durables	Total
San Pedro Sac.							
San Pedro	San Pedro	1941	7	Q348	Q 2	Q35	Q385
San Pedro	San Pedro	1955	24	359	28	37	424
San Pedro	Sr. Sepultado	1946	10	75	–	15	90
Aldea San José	San José	1969	5	104	2	–	106
Aldea San José	Sr. Sepultado	1955	14	59	6	–	65
Aldea San José	Virgen Rosario	1957	7	165	8	12	185
Cantón Sta. María	Niño de Atocha	1967	8	83	11	10	104
Aldea Chamac	San Isidro	1964	15	258	5	17	280
Aldea Chamac	San Isidro	1965	15	231	6	30	267
Aldea Petz	San Pedro	1954	6	115	22	–	187
Aldea Petz	San Pedro	1964	7	86	11	–	97
Aldea Petz	Santiago	1969	7	155	12	13	180
San Miguel Ixta.							
Aldea Subchal	Virgen Dolores	1955	14	138	50	–	188[a]
Aldea Subchal	Virgen Dolores	1959	15	100	38	2	140[a]
Aldea Subchal	Virgen Dolores	1960	14	115	36	5	156[a]
Aldea El Triunfo	Corpus Cristi	1966	4	52	18	–	70[b]
Aldea Xponá	Virgen Rosario	1964	3	31	6	–	37[b]

[a]Divided between four sponsors
[b]divided between two sponsors

branches of service are open: in the civil offices of the *alcaldía* (hamlet administration) and in the festive offices of the *templo*. As the local people explain it, each branch has its own kind of responsibilities, and some people feel themselves better suited to discharge one kind rather than the other. Religious service requires a concerted effort to accumulate a large reserve of food and money. Civil service entails much less material expense but is more time consuming, since the aldean mayor and his three councilmen must serve alternate weeks of duty at the alcaldía. It is also a more sensitive job. Civil officers must deal continually with town drunks (who, over time, include almost the entire population), and must always exercise good judgment since their performance can be reviewed by higher authorities and punished if found lacking.

Some men serve in both branches of public life; others in just one. Those who choose religious service do so spontaneously and voluntarily. Men regularly solicit posts, and the more expensive posts (those of San Pedro and Santiago) are the most popular. There is little tendency in the community to let one's obligations slide. Opulent service is considered to be estimable by participants and observers alike, but the amount spent is to some degree discretionary in all posts. The community expectation is not that a fiesta be celebrated lavishly, but that the obligation be met to the best of the sponsor's ability. *Según la capacidad de cada quien* (each according to his means) is a phrase commonly heard in Petz and also in the other aldeas of the township that still have individually sponsored fiestas. Ritual sponsorship, people here seem to feel, is an act of religious devotion as well as a social obligation, and should not be the exclusive privilege of the well-to-do. Thus some cofrades of more limited resources will candidly admit that their situation required them to host a relatively inexpensive festivity, while their wealthier neighbors boast of engaging an expensive double marimba band from San Pedro, complete with amplifying equipment. The community accepts both efforts.

Multiple service is not unusual. Seven men in the aldea have discharged more than one fiesta post. Informants agree, however, that multiple service is declining. In previous generations, *señores grandes* with outstanding cofradía careers were more numerous. The people explain this decline not as loss of *voluntad* but as a mathematical inevitability. Aldean population has increased noticeably, but the number of ritual posts is the same as it has always been. Opportunities for fiesta overachievement are consequently reduced.

Support of the traditional rituals is likewise strong among the Indians of the cabecera of Cucho, across the ravine from Petz. We still have *mucha voluntad*, the people say, we are still *católicos* here. By "católicos" they mean they are still Catholics by indigenous definition, supporters of Indian *costumbre* (religious tradition) as distinct from the *catequistas* who, in many other communities, have been converted to orthodox-Church doctrine. The orthodox Church has developed little influence in either Cucho or Petz.

There are seven Indian cofradías in Cucho, one of them being the duelo of El Señor Sepultado. Of the seven, five are still well supported; the cofradías of La Virgen Maria and of Concepción are "decaying." Fiestas for these two saints are still celebrated, but with decreasing pomp and expense. Sponsors used to slaughter pigs and calves for the fiestas; this is now rare, and sometimes even a marimba is lacking.

Support for the other fiestas is still strong and lavish. As in Petz, some men have served more than once, and it is not unusual for a family to host the vigil of El Señor Sepultado for up to five consecutive years, usually to fulfill a vow. One man, a carpenter and highly respected Indian leader, has twice served as cofrade of La Resurrección and is presently first councilman of the municipio. Shortly before my interview with him, he had been invited to sponsor the celebration of Santiago, one of the two most important fiestas in the community, and had decided to accept. He did so even though his previous service had more than fulfilled his community obligation and even though Santiago is one of the most expensive posts in the community system. In Cucho, he said, people still respect those who serve the images and this inspired him to continue participating. He recalled proudly that for his last service 400 villagers had joined the religious procession which carried the image to his home.

He has also participated in the *bailes mascarados* (masked dances) that volunteer groups often stage in conjunction with the festivities. These intricately choreographed dances are another aspect of the conspicuous giving associated with folk ritual in many communities. The men who stage them for the public to enjoy must rent costumes, hire musicians, and spend many hours in the months preceding the fiesta rehearsing their roles. Dances are still celebrated with some regularity in both Cucho and Petz. In 1970 they were preparing a *baile de conquista* (dance of the Conquest) in Cucho for the coming fiesta of the patron saint. It is generally conceded, however, that public enthusiasm for dance participation, like that for the sponsorship of certain cofradías, is on the wane.

The Indians of Cucho are somewhat more religiously conservative than those of Petz, since in Cucho they still support the *chimanes* (shamans), who have not been active in Petz for about 30 years. The chimanes in Cucho, although no longer commanding the political power they once had, are still influential in the cultural life of the Indian community. The head chimán, in fact, is so exalted and influential that he boasts a title, *el Timón del Pueblo* (the rudder of the community). The chimanes preside over all costumbre, rites of healing, life crises, and weather control. They also dictate many of the activities and expenditures of the cofrades and the Indian civil officers. The Indians support them staunchly. An ex-mayor of the town, a Ladino, attempted to eliminate the political costumbre of the Indian officials—the prayers, burning of *copal,* and sacrifice of turkeys by which Indians sanctify the exchange of authority. He was unsuccessful. He said the Indians told him he could do as he wished, but if he used his authority against the Timón del Pueblo they would refuse to participate in municipal government. Furthermore, the ex-mayor complained, the Indian officers select their own successors and always choose men who support the chimanes and the Timón del Pueblo.

It is difficult to say why the chimán institution has died out in Petz while in neighboring Cucho it still flourishes, but the explanation is probably political. During the reign of the dictator Ubico, *chimanería* was prohibited on the national level and all local agencies were ordered to prosecute the chimanes. In the centrally located cabecera of San Pedro, vigilance against chimán activities was fairly effective. Petz, though remote from the municipal cabecera, was under its direct political control. Aldean officials reported weekly to the municipal mayor, and the mayor and his officials occasionally visited outlying aldeas. San Cristóbal Cucho, on the other hand, has always been more independent; it has never had direct municipal ties to centers of authority in the urban zone, so its Indian institutions have been less vulnerable to outside influence. The same has been true of the interior communities, in all of which chimanes still operate.

In sum, fiesta organization in Petz and Cucho no longer has its pristine traditional form. The shamans have lost some of their political power in San Cristóbal Cucho and disappeared in San Pedro Petz, and support for certain cofradías and for dance participation is waning—a preview, perhaps, of more profound changes to come. But in these communities people still subscribe to the concept of conspicuous giving. Voluntary fiesta sponsorship is still the norm, cofrades are respected men, and no groups have emerged among the Indians with definable reasons for opposing ceremonial service or criticizing sponsors. Cucho and Petz are recognized in the entire region as strongholds of native costumbre, and the people of these communities are themselves quite aware of their conservatism. As the auxiliary mayor of Petz noted,

> In the cabecera San Pedro they no longer have cofrades. Now they only observe the processions. Previously there were many cofrades in San Pedro: there were *costumbres grandes* in the cabecera. But they have lost those customs while we still maintain them. Because we believe that if there are no cofrades the fiesta is not gay. When there are cofrades and bailes mascarados the fiesta is gay.

San Pedro

Fiesta customs in San Pedro used to be even more complex and opulent than those of Petz or Cucho, as befits a cabecera and major town. There were three classes of sponsored fiestas in the cabecera: general fiestas (which were actually fiestas of the entire municipio, though they were supported mainly by townspeople), Holy Week fiestas, and *cantón* or neighborhood fiestas. In all, ten major sponsored fiestas were celebrated in town each year.[1]

The three general festivities of San Pedro Apóstol, La Virgen de la Merced, and Corpus Cristi were the most lavish of the yearly round. All were of similar organization and were monumentally expensive, but that of San Pedro Apóstol was the most complex.

Each year the celebration of the municipal patron, for example, was the obligation of three men. First, the *cofrade mayor* held the major celebrations in his house, preceded by a novena (nine days of prayer culminating on the day of the saint), and succeeded by a night of vigil in the church. During the nine days of religious activity in his home, the cofrade mayor supplied food, drink, and music to hundreds of people. He was assisted in this labor by his *devotos*, friends or kin whose aid he had elicited. The principal devotos were the half-dozen or so *alcaldes de cohetes* (fireworks officials), each of whom donated to the festivities twelve dozen skyrockets and twenty-five pounds of gunpowder for making *bombas*. Each alcalde also had a number of assistants who helped him shoot off the rockets throughout the nights of celebration. Other devotos contributed to the mass stipend on the saint's day (usually around Q50, being a high mass), while still others contributed the fee of the marimba orchestra. The cofrade, in turn, was obligated to recognize the aid of each devoto with a ceremonial *repuesto,* commonly a gift of a large basket of festive bread and chocolate.

The *velada de andas* (vigil of the litter), which preceded the celebration of the cofrade mayor, was sponsored by a second individual, who had the duty of decorating and adoring the image and the litter on which it would later be carried in procession. This person's expenses were less than those of the cofrade mayor, but were nonetheless significant since he was expected to purchase the decorations for the litter and to feed the guests who attended his vigil.

Finally, after the major festivity, another sequence of prayers was hosted by a third man, the *cofrade de la octava,* who was actually the incoming cofrade mayor. The octava consisted of eight days of prayers, which he hosted in his home, followed as usual by refreshments for the participants. These three men, the cofrade mayor, the celebrant of the anda, and the cofrade de la octava, along with their counterparts from the cofradías of La Virgen de la Merced and Corpus Cristi, composed a cooperating religious body of nine men who attended one another's celebrations, marched in one another's processions, and represented the community as a whole before its major deities for a period of one year.

Since San Pedro Apóstol was the patron saint of the entire township, his fiesta was also enlivened by the coronation of queens, public dances, and athletic competitions. These events were organized by a *comité festejo* (festive committee) appointed by municipal authorities, and were financed out of the municipal treasury. Organization of the fiesta in its entirety was thus divided between the cofradía and the comité, the former charged with sacred events and the latter with secular events. The other fiestas of the cabecera differed only in size and minor detail from the fiesta of San Pedro. The municipality participated only in the fiesta patronal. Holy Week cofradías, such as Jesús Nazareno and El Señor Sepultado, were less expensive, being duelos, and had ritual content re-enacting the biblical history of Christ's final days. Cantón festivities were replicas of the general cofradías with a cofrade mayor, velada de andas, and comité festejo, but in miniature, since they pertained to residential segments of the town only. The big fiesta of Corpus Cristi was also traditionally enlivened by elaborate masked dances and by the irreverent antics of disguised pranksters who ran about teasing and molesting people in the streets.

This entire complex of public rituals existed in the memory of all adult San Pedranos, and had been supported by some of them. It was once a well-supported system in which the honor of sponsorship was *solicitado, hasta peleado* (requested, even fought over). Now it has virtually disappeared: masked dance groups no longer perform; sponsor posts are never requested for the major festivities and rarely for the cantón celebrations; and the previously important images of La Virgen de la Merced and Corpus Cristi are now observed by a dwindling clique of elderly people, who still honor them with a small procession and a night of prayer.

Public festivities, which are as numerous and as grand as ever, are now run either by hermandades—large religious clubs formally associated with the orthodox Church, administered by elected officials, and supported by the collection of dues—or in the cantones by ad hoc committees, the old comités festejos, which have expanded their activities to include the hosting of vigils that individuals are no longer inspired to sponsor. Even the great fiesta of San Pedro, the patron of the entire township, is so organized. To most San Pedranos, the idea of ritual sponsorship, a role honored and coveted by their parents and ancestors back to the sixteenth century, has become an embarrassment or at best a nuisance, a cultural anachronism to be replaced by something more acceptably modern.

The trend of ritual change in San Pedro differs from that of Petz and Cucho. In those rustic communities we noted that certain ritual events were declining in the public estimation, as though they had passed out of fashion. The idea of ritual sponsorship, however, is still upheld—cofrades are still forthcoming and there has been no attempt to replace traditional participation with something else. In San Pedro, by contrast, the concept of conspicuous ritual giving has been rejected over the last few decades, the motivations behind it have dissipated, and the indigenous organizations have been superseded by totally new forms of association.

San Miguel Ixtahuacán

The history of ritual change in San Miguel Ixtahuacán begins earlier and is more complicated than that of the communities just discussed. There has been a distinct trend in San Miguel toward reduction of individual costs of participation, just as there was in San Pedro, but the nature of the change and its underlying stimuli are different. In San Pedro the tendency toward conspicuous ritual giving declined as the community grew wealthier and more sophisticated, and indigenous cofradías were replaced with complex "administered" organizations. In San Miguel, the resistence to fiesta sponsorship intensified as the community economy degenerated, and it centered not so much on the concept of giving as on the traditional *rate* of ritual expenditure.

The traditional ceremonial system in San Miguel was highly centralized until the 1930s. All cofrades were appointed by the municipal authorities and the major festive events took place in the cabecera. Eleven images were honored with feasts every year, the same number as the number of aldeas in the municipio, including the cabecera. In this early period, however, the images did not pertain to particular aldeas. They were housed in the colonial church in the cabecera, and sponsors were drawn from the population at large, with no attempt to match particular saints to sponsors from particular aldeas.

Two cofrades, a "first" and a "second," were appointed for each image. The appointments were made by the political officials of the municipio under the direction of the municipal mayor, with supernatural ratification by a head chimán. The appointees were notified by the auxiliary mayors of the aldeas in which they lived. The officials made some attempt to distribute appointments equitably. They would meet in conference to discuss those men economically and morally qualified to accept cargos and to choose among those who still owed service to the community.

The traditional system in San Miguel was distinct in two ways from those we have already discussed. First, it was more centralized. In San Pedro Sacatepéquez and in San Cristóbal Cucho, each community—cabecera, aldea, or neighborhood—supported its own independent festivities. In none of these cases was the entire township ever integrated into a single ritual system. In these communities, furthermore, outgoing sponsors searched for their own replacements without intervention or interest on the part of political authorities. Second, the interconnection of religious and political life in San Miguel lent the ceremonial system an added measure of conservatism. Municipal ex-mayors agreed that it was their duty to help preserve the ancient customs by forcing reluctant sponsor nominees to accept their cargos. Ceremonial participation in San Miguel was always underlain by an element of formal coercion that did not exist in the other communities; service was *obligatorio*. This does not mean that there was no spontaneous commitment to the native ceremonials and that all sponsors had to be forced. Some men accepted nomination willingly, but the mayors could jail those who did not.

The municipio of San Miguel traditionally observed a yearly cycle of ceremonials in honor of *each* saint. Three of these ceremonials were group events involving most cofradías: Holy Week, Corpus Cristi in June, and the fiesta of the municipal patron, San Miguel Arcángel, in September. Each cofradía celebrated a vigil with feasting, music, dancing, and fireworks in its *casa de cofradía* in the cabecera, and participated in religious processions. Another individual event was observed yearly by each cofradía on its saint's day in order to celebrate the saint's day and to sanctify the replacement of cofrades. Generally, this was a smaller ceremony attended only by the families of the principals involved.

Each cofradía, then, was responsible for a series of ceremonials each year, and each cofrade paid his own share. The community did not financially assist the sponsors: "the expenses came out of the ribs of the cofrades." Chimanes directed all ritual—familial and political as well as cofradía. For the cofradías, the chimanes provided the necessary esoteric ritual knowledge. They "seated" the cofrades at the beginning of each event, "raised" them at its conclusion, and performed all the sacrifices that came in between. Participation by Catholic priests was minimal. Baptismal records indicate that there was no resident priest in the community between 1906 and 1957. Priests from Tejutla were invited to say mass on the three major religious dates, but they stayed close to the church, never attempted a serious program of conversion, and never interfered with the activities in the casas de cofradía where the chimanes reigned supreme. Both the priests and the chimanes were given money and food by the cofrades, in payment for their services.

This system remained intact until the dictator Ubico assumed national power in the 1930s and replaced municipal mayors with his own men. These appointees (*intendentes*) controlled all municipios, served for unspecified lengths of time, and were answerable only to higher officials. The first intendente assigned to San Miguel was a local man who was removed shortly after assuming office. The second was a Ladino outsider who, by fiat, reorganized the community fiesta system. His reasons for doing so are unclear. Some say he thought the native system was poorly organized. Perhaps, being an outsider, he found the job of fitting local personalities into ceremonial posts beyond his capability. Whatever his reason, he distributed the municipio's images among the aldeas, assigning one to each, and delegated to each hamlet the responsibility for recruiting its own cofrades and organizing its own festivities. Cabajchúm became responsible for the image of San Miguel Aparición, Subchal for the Virgen de Dolores, El Zapote for San Jerónimo, Chílibe for La Asunción de la Virgen, the cabecera for San Miguel Arcángel, and so on. This fractionalized system was continued even after Ubico was deposed and municipal administration returned to local people. The original organization was never revived.

It was after reorganization of the system by the intendente that festive activity began to show definite signs of decline in San Miguel. The municipal system declined at varying rates and in varying ways in different aldeas, but decline has been steady, clear, and continuous. Communal festivities are now greatly attenuated compared to those of the earlier period. Corpus Cristi passes unsung, few aldeas participate in the fiesta of San Miguel Arcángel, and several aldeas have eliminated feasting, dancing, and fireworks, celebrating the day of their saint with a mass only. Three aldeas have had their images stolen and have not bothered to replace them or to continue group rituals of any kind. Chimanes in San Miguel are not generally respected, as they are in Cucho, nor were they eliminated during the Ubico oppression as they were in Petz and San Pedro. Their influence and numbers are waning because, like the cofradías, they are losing popular support.

Because changes in regional society and economy have altered people's perceptions of costs and benefits of community ritual, support for this activity is declining throughout highland San Marcos. Chapters 7 through 8 discuss the recent histories of San Miguel Ixtahuacán and San Pedro, describing the new conditions which led these people to reorganize their ceremonial life.

Notes

[1] The principal cofradías of the town of San Pedro were as follows:

General cofradías	Cantón cofradías	Holy Week cofradías
San Pedro Apóstol	El Niño de Atocha	Jesús Nazareno
La Virgen de la Merced	San Sebastián	El Señor Sepultado
Corpus Cristi	San Miguel	
	San Augustín	
	San Juan de Dios	

The feast days of Corazón de Jesús, Jesús de la Humildad, and la Virgen de Dolores (all Holy Week images) were also celebrated, but did not have formal cofradías. These images resided in the central church and were taken out by whoever had the voluntad to pay for a novena and mass. Each of these fiestas is presently celebrated by an hermandad.

SEVEN

San Miguel Ixtahuacán: Agrarian Crisis in an Indian Municipio

San Miguel Ixtahuacán is an anomaly, an Indian community that is rejecting its Indian ceremonials. A basic reason for this ritual breakdown is that San Miguel is no longer "peasant" in the economic sense of being a self-sufficient group marginally involved in the market. San Miguel is Indian in its culture, language, and identity, but it is far from self-sufficient, since it is now heavily dependent on finca labor and coastal corn to carry it through the year. This growing involvement in the cash sector is the Indians' attempt to compensate for dislocations in their traditional subsistence system. It is an indicator of economic decline and of the reduction in the surpluses consumed during fiestas.

This chapter discusses the relationship of San Miguel's agrarian crisis to population growth in the highlands and the expansion of cash agriculture on the Pacific coast. This necessitates a historical approach, which is a risky endeavor in view of the scarcity of records in this preliterate community. The idea of a peasant-to-proletarian economic devolution is nevertheless the best conceptualization of what we can discover about San Miguel's recent history.

Before the development of coastal coffee plantations, Indian populations in San Marcos must have been highly self-reliant, since at that time there were few outside sources of wage labor. Before the road-building efforts of Ubico, furthermore, the entire highland region of San Marcos was more isolated than it is now. Even the twin cities were without good connections in those days. All travel was by foot and horse, so it was impossible for interior municipios to be provisioned with outside goods to the present extent.

San Miguel has been losing this independence throughout the century. Miguelenses were involved in finca labor by the early 1900s and appear to have grown progressively dependent on the plantations ever since. In the 1960s they began working the cotton as well as the coffee harvests. They now purchase much of their food and all of their clothing. Barter, a common means of exchange in the memory of older men, has been completely supplanted by money. Roads that were cut in the 1960s from Tejutla to Concepción Tutuapa and San Miguel opened the area to outside goods and to commerce, increasing Miguelense dependence even more.

Wage and market involvement has been accompanied by rapid population growth, and a general decline of the community's economic situation, two processes that are occurring broadly among Guatemala's Indians. At 3.3 percent per year, Guatemala has one of the highest population growth rates in the world. National population quadrupled between 1821 and 1921, and almost tripled in the following 50 years. In the 1960s, national economic growth lagged far behind population and inflation, with most benefits accruing to the upper classes (James 1969:130-31, 141-42). Guatemala's rich are growing richer, while her poor, especially the rural poor and most especially the seasonal laborers, are growing poorer. "It is hard," Adams writes, "to avoid the conclusion that the Guatemalan *campesino* receives an extraordinarily low income and that it is probable this income has decreased during the past fifteen years" (1970:393, see also James 1969:141).

The Present Perspective

San Miguel Ixtahuacán lies in a zone of rugged mountains, four hours by bus into the interior from the twin cities. Ixtahuacán, as the cabecera of the municipio is called, nestles in a beautiful valley at approximately the geographic center of the township. East of the cabecera the land slopes downward and the Indians plant oranges and a small amount of coffee in addition to corn. To the southeast the terrain rises and the Indians raise corn, wheat, oats, and small number of sheep. The terrain is very broken and, in the lower regions, rocky; flat land is scarce and foot travel arduous.

The poverty here is extreme even by rural Guatemalan standards. There are signs of soil destruction everywhere—hillsides scarred with ugly red gashes where even weeds do not grow. Houses are small and crowded, and people dress in old, patched clothes. In late August and September Indians fill truck after truck; whole families—men, women, schoolchildren, and

TABLE II
San Miguel Ixtahuacán: Domestic Expenditures
Of Five Families, 1969 (in quetzals)

Family Size	Food	Clothing	Farm Costs*	Medicine	Total
9	91.00	30.00	53.54	4.00	178.54
5	114.00	28.00	29.36	9.00	176.36
5	117.00	40.00	32.36	9.00	208.36
3	52.00	30.00	70.46	1.75	154.21
6	52.00	50.00	88.13	3.50	193.63

*Includes expenditures for seed, fertilizer, tools, rental of land, and all other farm costs.

infants—embark on the long trip to coastal coffee fincas. At the height of the coffee harvest, the municipio is virtually vacant, its citizens off sweating for others' profit.

Most houses are one-room huts of adobe or wattle with hard-packed dirt floors, averaging about 400 square feet of floor space. Into these small dwellings are packed one and sometimes two or three families. A separate, windowless hut serves as a kitchen. Women spend much of their lives in these kitchens, squatting around the open fire or grinding corn for the monotonous Indian diet. Corn tortillas or tamalitos and beans, spiced with chile sauce, are the staples. Most families have meat about once a week, some much less frequently.

Except for seasonal agricultural labor, San Miguel has little to sell in the national market. The lower aldeas export small quantities of peaches and oranges, and Sícabe, a high aldea with good rolling land, produces a small surplus of wheat. Crude porous pottery is made by many families of the aldeas of Máquivil, Subchal, and La Patria. No other commodities are sold to the outside in any quantity. Family incomes and domestic budgets are consequently small. Families rarely spend more than Q200 to maintain themselves and their households over the year. Table II presents domestic accounts for five farm families in 1969. These families spent about Q30 per person for the year. By far the largest expenditures were for food. Although Miguelenses value the consumer goods now available in the shops of San Pedro, they can afford few of them. Surveying 24 aldean households, I found only six radios, three clocks, one treadle sewing machine, and one typewriter. The sewing machine, typewriter, and one radio all belonged to a finca labor recruiter. Most families have no luxury goods.

There are no firms, consumer unions, or cooperatives in the municipio. Only an occasional farmer takes advantage of the credit facilities of the National Wheat Growers' Union or of the banks in San Marcos; few, in fact, are aware of the credit programs these institutions offer. Families produce, buy, and sell independently and competitively, and even traditional exchange labor has been supplanted by wages. Although farmers regularly hire their neighbors to help with soil preparation or wheat threshing, there is not, to my knowledge, a single individual within the township who hires labor on a permanent basis. Prices respond to supply and demand only. The government's attempt to control the price of wheat has been subverted by free-lance truckers from San Pedro. Ignorant of the official price, Indians are an easy target for exploitation.

Twenty years ago most Miguelenses were completely untutored because there was only one grammer school in the township. Now there is a teacher in each aldea, and the cabecera school offers complete primary education. The major effect of these new facilities has been to improve basic literacy and to increase peoples' awareness of national history, civic institutions, and political leaders. Education has not provided the community with economically worthwhile information or inspired new ambitions. Miguelenses view education more as a means of self-protection than as a basis for social advance. Parents often told me the value of schooling is so their children will know the basic arithmetic and Spanish they need to "defend their rights" against outsiders. Educational trends and attitudes are clearly exposed in Table III, which presents final examination results for all students in the municipio in 1968. The table distinguishes between educational accomplishments in the main school in Ixtahuacán (the cabecera) and the eleven schools in the aldeas. *Castellanización* refers to the first year of instruction, which is devoted strictly to Spanish grammar and vocabulary. All teachers who specialize in rural education are trained to teach castellanización. As the table shows, girls receive less instruction than boys. In almost all grades in all schools, fewer girls than boys are enrolled, and they tend to drop out faster. Aldean children spend less time in school than children residing in Ixtahuacán; in the Ladinoized cabecera, children learn Spanish before beginning school and stay enrolled longer. The number of students drops consistently as one proceeds up the grades, the most significant decline occurring between third and fourth grades. The dropout and failure rate is very high.

TABLE III

San Miguel Ixtahuacán: Final Exam Results, All Schools, 1968

Grades	Boys				Girls				Totals	
	Enroll	Pass	Fail	Absent	Enroll	Pass	Fail	Absent	Enroll	Pass
Ixtahuacán: Coed "Urban" School										
Castellanización	0									
First	34	28	3	3	18	14	1	3	52	42
Second	34	28	6	0	7	6	0	1	41	34
Third	17	11	2	4	5	4	1	0	22	15
Fourth	10	3	0	7	8	6	0	2	18	9
Fifth	9	6	1	2	4	4	0	0	13	10
Sixth	6	6	0	0	5	5	0	0	11	11
Aldeas: Eleven Coed "Rural" Schools										
Castellanización	143	89	12	42	65	23	7	35	208	112
First	151	77	20	64	61	16	13	32	222	93
Second	106	71	13	22	16	5	3	8	122	76
Third	76	27	2	47	4	3	0	1	80	30
Fourth	15	6	0	9	4	4	0	0	19	10
Fifth	3	1	0	2	1	1	0	0	4	2
Sixth	1	1	0	0	1	0	0	1	2	1

This limited educational interest is rooted in economic conditions over which local people have no control. An aldean child can attend school only up to third grade in his hamlet. To complete primary school he would have to commute to the municipal cabecera, and to earn a high-school degree—which would significantly expand his occupational possibilities—he would have to move to San Marcos or San Pedro. This is well beyond the reach of virtually all Miguelenses. Only 14 Indians from San Miguel have secondary degrees, and all of them have come from five of the community's wealthiest families. Scholarships for promising students are rare. Besides, from an early age, children make real contributions to the family by working alongside their parents at home and on the plantations. For most parents this assistance takes precedence over schooling.

Population Growth

Rapid population growth is the single most important fact in the recent history of San Miguel Ixtahuacán. Women in San Miguel begin reproducing at a young age and continue till quite old, and families are large. I gathered census data on 119 families in four San Miguel aldeas and comparative information on 27 families in San Cristóbal Cucho (see Table IV). The 146 mothers in this sample have produced a total of 1346 offspring, over nine per mother. More important, they are radically overcompensating for child mortality, which is about 25 percent in the entire sample. For mothers 45 years old and younger, hamlet averages for living children vary between 4.0 and 5.5; for mothers over 45 the range is 4.5 to 7.2. A significant percentage of infants is born to women who in developed countries would be considered too young or too old for childbearing. The youngest mother in the sample reported her age as 16, the oldest as 50.

The causes of this population upsurge are complex and require further study, but two factors stand out as obviously important. First, public health programs do more to control mortality in these villages than to control fertility. The public health nurses stationed in each municipio regularly launch vaccination campaigns and administer medicine for intestinal parasites in mass programs, but they do no work in family planning—the unmarried nurse in San Miguel herself bore two children during the period I studied the community. The departmental health clinic in San Marcos does run an understaffed birth control service, but it has had little effect in nearby communities, much less in the remote interior.

TABLE IV

Fertility Statistics, San Migual Ixtahuacán and San Cristóbal Cucho

	Subchal	Chilibe	Sícabe	Triunfo	SMI Totals	San Cristóbal Cucho
Mothers in sample	19	30	30	40	119	27
Mothers' ave. age	43.1	41.8	39.1	37.4	39.8	44.2
Total births	167	282	316	325	1090	256
Mo. 45 and under	64%	70%	63%	75%	69%	56%
Total births	108	212	214	247	781	164
No. living children	62	148	164	159	533	115
Ave. no. living children	3.3	4.9	5.5	4.0	4.5	4.3
Mo. over 45	36%	30%	37%	25%	31%	44%
Total births	59	70	102	78	309	92
No. living children	33	48	79	45	205	58
Ave. no. living children	4.7	5.3	7.2	4.5	5.5	4.8

The second and more important cause of population growth is that the labor requirements of the local economy promote large families. Because San Miguel is a labor-intensive community, children are an asset both in the fields and on the fincas. They are also the only source of old-age security. Parents, when they become too old for heavy work, demand that their children look after them, and have been known to enforce this demand with threats of disinheritance. From the point of view of the parents, who actually determine family size, large families are beneficial.

Population and Soil Fertility

Growing population pressure has disrupted food production in San Miguel by interfering with traditional methods of soil fertilization. Miguelenses are high-altitude farmers who scratch their living from an uncooperative environment. Mountains are not the ideal place to grow corn, since it takes almost twice as long to mature as on the hot humid coast. Furthermore, almost all arable land in San Miguel is steep, and constant rejuvenation is essential. Farmers previously maintained soil fertility through application of garbage and manure, and, more important, through fallowing.

Land immediately surrounding houses receives the constant benefit of kitchen wastes, animal droppings, and human excrement. This land was and is the Indian's most productive and can be continually cultivated, but it amounts to less than a third of an acre per household. Animal manure is always carefully stored and applied to the crop at the time of planting or shortly thereafter. Indians everywhere go to considerable effort to collect manure. In San Pedro, after the big market day, people living next to incoming trails assiduously collect the droppings of passing mule trains. Market officials in San Miguel receive as their only remuneration the right to collect manure from around the plaza. I have seen men who live over an hour's walk from the plaza make repeated trips to their homes carrying heavy bags of raw manure strapped to their heads.

Rotation of sheep corrals is another native fertilization technique. Sheep are penned at night inside a square corral made of corn stalks. After a few days, during which their droppings and urine soak the soil and are tilled in by the animals' sharp hooves, the corral is moved to a new location. Since land so fertilized produces high yields for several years, this technique is common in sheep-raising municipios throughout the highlands.

In the fertile valley around San Pedro, plots produce continually with no fertilization other than application of wastes in the ways just described. Farmers in San Pedro can point out fields that have been under constant cultivation for at least 40 years. In the mountainous interior around San Miguel, the land is rarely so fertile. Since there were not sufficient wastes to maintain all cultivated land, farmers were forced to periodically fallow most of their plots. Land would be allowed to rest from two to 12 or more years, depending on the amount of land the farmer owned and on his needs. After fallowing, the vegetation, sometimes brush, sometimes tall clump grass called *pajón,* was cut and burned. Land fertilized with burned vegetation would produce for two to three years, with yields decreasing each year.

In the 1930s Stadelman studied slash-and-burn cultivation in the department of Huehuetenango, noting that "fertilization, both in Todos Santos and other sheep-raising districts of the country, is recognized by the Indians as the salvation of the soil, without which the highlands would soon become useless for maize cultivation" (1940:104). He concluded that slash-and-burn was an effective, long-term practice for maintaining the maize-producing potential of highland soils (1940:109, 117). The destruction of timber was unfortunate and promoted some leaching, but cutting and burning was still the most economical method of clearing land. It introduced significant quantities of organic matter and minerals into the soil, loosened the soil, and freed it of all insect pests and vermin. Stadelman also left no doubt about the long-term utility of the practice. There is some loss of effectiveness as timber gives way to brush and finally to grasses after successive burnings. Longer fallowing periods then become necessary, but no land is ever rendered permanently sterile as a result of slash-and-burn fertilization.

Because of population expansion, however, traditional fertilization techniques of corral rotation and swidden fallowing are now virtually obsolete in San Miguel. Old men remember when they were common, but now few have sufficient land to allow plots to lie dormant long enough to regenerate sufficient brush. Land shortages and *minifundismo* are now the rule. Constant use has led to soil exhaustion and to a significant reduction in yields. "The land used to be powerful; it was new," one old man said. Another stood at his front door explaining that when he was young there were "many open lands, with big trees." He gestured toward the terrain surrounding his house, now solidly planted with small plots of corn and wheat, saying it had previously been open. People had more land in those days, he said, and more animals. Now they even have to keep their chickens tied up for fear they will ruin a neighbor's milpa.

To make matters worse, much land has been lost to erosion (see also Collier 1975:109-24). A soil expert who visited the community while I was there explained that the character of the soil, as well as the Indian practice of planting corn on steep hillsides, accounts for the severe erosion in the surrounding highlands. A large zone in northern San Marcos and southern Huehuetenango is underlain with an impermeable subsoil called *talpetate,* which reduces the capacity of the soil to absorb rainfall and causes destructive runoff when natural vegetation is removed. Erosion is not a recent problem. Old men say that the hillsides have been scarred for as long as they can remember, which indicates how extensively land was used even before recent population growth.

Erosion damage, however, has probably worsened as the growing population has expanded onto marginal land. Population movement can be detected in house surveys, since aldean houses endure for generations. A survey of aldea Subchal showed that of the 153 houses presently standing in the aldea, 92 had been built since the 1920s. Of the 61 houses that made up the hamlet in the 1920s, almost half are located on a small plain that is the only flat land in the vicinity. Subsequent buildings are located on steeper, less productive, and more erosion-prone terrain.

The effects of population expansion on landholdings have been further exacerbated by local inheritance rules. The Miguelense custom is for parents to divide their holdings among all their children. Daughters as well as sons inherit property, although usually in smaller proportion. The quality of plots is taken into account in the division, so a son receiving choice land usually receives less quantity than his siblings. The parents' house customarily goes to the eldest son unless he has been derelict in supporting his father and mother in their old age, in which case it is given to the most attentive child. Land inherited by daughters is theirs exclusively and does not come under their husband's control. As a result of this inheritance pattern, estates have been divided and redivided, and individual holdings are usually broadly dispersed. Men commonly work plots two or three hours walk from their place of residence. Providing each offspring with a plot, however small and fragmentary, also tends to reduce emigration by tying people to the local area.

Since there are few opportunities that would draw people permanently out of the municipio or into nonagricultural occupations, land has become not only scarce but expensive as well. Men complain that even if one accumulates money to buy land, few are willing to sell. Almost no one has a surplus, and those who do are guarding it for their children. Land prices have risen considerably over the last 30 years, which local farmers offer as evidence of land scarcity. One pointed out a 13-*cuerda*[1] plot he purchased in 1945 and an 18-cuerda plot he obtained in 1962. Though they are adjacent, identical in quality, and of similar size, the latter cost him three times as much as the former. Land was previously so plentiful that men sold lots without even measuring them; the buyer and seller would merely mark out the parcel and haggle over its price. Now everything is carefully measured and sold by the unit.

Population and Farm Size

This descriptive account of agrarian crisis is borne out statistically. I surveyed a large sample of Miguelense farmers in seven aldeas to discover how the land situation has changed over the last generation. Farmers were asked about their own holdings and those of their fathers. The sample included 94 sons responding on themselves and their 92 fathers (see Table V).

This survey is most meaningful when compared to land statistics gathered by Wagley in Santiago Chimaltenango in 1937. Chimaltenango, in Huehuetenango, is also a Mam community located at approximately the same altitude as San Miguel. The two communities are so close, only 16 miles apart, that at the time of Wagley's study traders from Tutuapa regularly sold San Miguel pottery in Chimaltenango. At that time, the Indians of Chimaltenango were milperos using traditional slash-and-burn techniques. The community was involved in finca labor but exported a sizable corn surplus and supported a stable fiesta system. How did the Chimaltenango economy compare with that of San Miguel a generation ago and today?

Before Wagley's study, Chimaltenango had changed from corporate to private land tenure, which provoked marked disparity in wealth. Some Chimaltecos had sufficient land to mount semicommercial farming operations, hiring field help and producing significant surpluses. The most entrepreneurial of these purchased mules with their corn profits, hired themselves out as muleteers to coffee plantations, and plowed these profits back into the land. Other men owning little or no land were dependent on rentals and coffee wages for subsistence.

Wagley found that to be economically independent a family had to have access to at least 120 cuerdas of land. The family could then plant 60 cuerdas each year and fallow the rest, thereby producing sufficient maize for subsistence plus a surplus to exchange for other necessities. Given the productivity

TABLE V

Generational Change in Farm Size, San Miguel and Chimaltenango

	San Miguel* Present Generation N = 94	San Miguel Fathers N = 92	Chimaltenango 1937 N = 253
Average Farm Size (cuerdas)	67	119	101.5
Percent Farming 120 cuerdas or More	11%	28%	21%
Total Holdings (cuerdas)	6,325	10,898	25,688

*All respondents are sons who have received their entire inheritance. Figures also include land purchased by sons outside their inheritance. Finca labor recruiters were not included in the survey.

of the land and the standard of living of the village, 120 cuerdas was a "rock-bottom minimum" for maintaining a peasant adaptation and avoiding finca labor (Wagley 1941:55).

As can be seen from Table V, San Miguel was slightly better off than Chimaltenango a generation ago: the average farm was larger than that of Chimaltenango and a somewhat larger percentage of men farmed 120 cuerdas or more. But men who presently complain of a land shortage are right; over the last generation the average farm size has dropped dramatically, and the proportion of men who own at least 120 cuerdas has fallen to less than half its previous level. It is also significant that only 44 percent of the men in the San Miguel survey have managed to purchase land to supplement their inheritance.

Besides reducing per capita holdings, population pressure has cut farm income by reducing available pasturage and number of animals. There are presently fewer animal products (meat and wool) for people to consume and sell. Supplies of vital manure have also declined. A 70-year-old man, ex-mayor of the township, said that when he was young fewer people had to work on fincas. The land produced, he said, "because there were great flocks of sheep. Not like now. Farming used to be worthwhile but now the land does not respond." Elsewhere the refrain is similar. In El Triunfo a farmer noted that the only animals presently more abundant are mules, because nowadays more men are traders. The cattle butcher claims he rarely finds local beef, and almost all the steers he slaughters are trucked up from the coast. Another man remembers that when he was young (in the 1920s) 10 men in his aldea owned 26 oxen among them; now four men own a total of four oxen.

Rapid population growth in a stagnant economy based on extensive land use is doubly destructive. Not only does the demand for food increase as the number of people grows, but there can come a time when excessive pressure on local resources renders inoperative some vital component of their productive system. The population of San Miguel apparently reached reached a crisis generation, a point where people became so numerous that they could no longer employ slash-and-burn fertilization. Miguelenses report that slash-and-burn farming used to yield about 100 pounds of corn per cuerda, slightly more on exceptional or well-fallowed land. These returns are comparable to those recorded by Stadelman and Wagley. As population pressure increased in San Miguel, yields began to drop, reportedly falling to as low as one quarter of their earlier level. Only the recent introduction of chemical fertilizers has slowed this trend.

Although industrial fertilizers have become available in the last few years, they have not solved the production problem. Quantitative data from two aldeas show that Miguelenses are still highly reliant on purchased corn. Sícabe is a relatively prosperous hamlet and Chílibe a relatively impoverished one by San Miguel standards. Of thirty Sícabe families, 40 percent had purchased corn in 1969, averaging 470 pounds each. Of thirty families in Chílibe, 93 percent purchased corn, averaging 560 pounds each. Five hundred pounds of corn represents approximately 40 percent of a family's yearly consumption, and cost about Q20 in 1969. There were no corn-selling families in the Chílibe sample, and in Sícabe only four families sold corn the preceding season. Sícabe has the best wheat land in the municipio, and 67 percent of its sample families sold wheat. In Chílibe only 23 percent sold wheat.

The other aldeas of San Miguel are agriculturally more like Chílibe than Sícabe, which enjoys the most abundant, flattest terrain in the municipio. Corn is the principal crop and staple food in all aldeas, but no aldea produces enough to meet its needs.

Plaza Trade and Wage Labor

Faced with declining agricultural resources, Indians of San Miguel have become increasingly involved in plaza trade and plantation labor. Both are mere survival adaptations; neither provides sufficient income for savings or

capital expansion (Adams 1970:391). For the community as a whole, plantation labor is a much more important source of income. Trade is a limited
specialty practiced primarily by men from aldeas El Triunfo and Subchal.

Miguelenses engage in two forms of trade: smuggling and legal plaza
commerce. A small number of adventurous men are *contrabandistas* who
make regular trips to Comitán, Mexico, to smuggle Mexican medicines.
Except for finca labor recruiters, smugglers are the only men in the township
who have accumulated significant capital. Anacleto Díaz is one of the more
successful contrabandistas. Orphaned and destitute, he began smuggling at
age 18 and is now one of the wealthiest men in the township. He owns several
hundred cuerdas of land, a house with a tin roof, and a peddling inventory
worth around Q150. He has accumulated sufficient reserves to make regular
loans in the community, and on his trips to Mexico he now takes along young
men as porters. Anacleto is highly respected for his industry and courage. "If
we were all as *inteligente* as that *muchacho,*" one of his friends said, "none
of us would have to go to the fincas."

The trip to Comitán, however, is arduous. Most of the journey must be
made on foot and at night, rivers must be forded, there is little food, and
exposure is extreme. Besides, almost all smugglers sooner or later land in jail,
so smuggling is not as attractive to most men as legal plaza commerce. A few
Miguelenses founded legal *ventas* (mobile plaza stalls) during the period of
"liberty," as they call it, following the fall of Ubico. Many more established
themselves as peddlers after the Tejutla-San Miguel road was cut, and wares
became easier to purchase. Miguelenses presently operate over 80 stalls in the
Saturday plaza in El Triunfo, and some also trade in the big plaza of
Concepción Tutuapa and the smaller markets in the cabecera of Ixtahuacán.

Popular though it is, plaza commerce provides little income.
Miguelenses are too poor to purchase stock in bulk or transport it over long
distances, which are the major sources of commercial profits. Many comerciantes even purchase and sell their wares in the same plaza, so their profit
margins are minuscule. Since Miguelenses are also the most numerous participants in the commercial network, competition among them is extreme.
Surveying the El Triunfo plaza, I found 82 Miguelense-operated ventas
selling only 12 classes of merchandise. A man wishing to sell clothing would
have to compete with 32 other operators; to sell hardware, with 34 others; to
sell sugar and salt, with 25 others. Older comerciantes view the new road with
mixed feelings, since prior to its construction trade was a more limited
specialty. There were fewer traders, less outside merchandise entered the

community, and returns were higher. "Now there is more of everything—and less profit," one comerciante complained. But he added that the road and vehicles have eased the burden of trade; "We earn less now, but we aren't killing ourselves either."

Miguelenses have been blocked at every turn in their attempts to cope with population pressure. They have depleted their agricultural resources and are not profiting in any significant way from recent commercial developments in their region. Their only economic recourse has been the coastal farms, where their labor is in great demand.

Coffee may have been introduced into Guatemala in colonial times, but commercial production did not begin until the latter half of the nineteenth century. The government exempted coffee from all taxes in 1879, adding momentum to its production, and by the turn of the century the crop was well established as the nation's leading export. In 1911, productivity for the first time exceeded 100 million pounds; in 1931, coastal San Marcos was the major coffee-producing region in the country, with about one-fifth of the national total (Jones 1940:203-8).

In the absence of records it is difficult to establish a precise history of Miguelense involvement in coffee labor, but it is likely that their dependence on this source of income has increased steadily throughout this century, probably approaching maximum during the forced-labor epoch of Ubico.

The present-day labor exodus from San Miguel is as heavy as in any community I am familiar with. Virtually every adult in the township has done coastal labor at some time in his life; most families depend on it yearly. I made quantitative estimates of labor involvement in three aldeas. In Sícabe, the most prosperous Miguelense hamlet, of thirty families 67 percent reported doing coastal work the preceding year, averaging 76 man-days per family. In the poorer aldea of Chílibe, 77 percent of thirty families had done field labor, averaging 89 man-days per family. Eighteen of 19 families in aldea Subchal reported working on coffee or cotton plantations (sometimes both) the preceding year. These families averaged 73 man-days of work. At the peak of the coffee season I checked every house in Subchal, finding 73 percent vacant. Most of the others were occupied by one or two family members who had been left behind because of illness or to keep watch on the fields.

When the labor recruiters return from the fincas early in the year carrying advance money to contract workers, they find men waiting at their doors to sign on. Some families receive so many advances that they are paid in full even before leaving for the coast, and work only to discharge their contract.

Recent involvement of Miguelenses in cotton labor implies that wage dependence has grown even over the last decade. Cotton is a relatively new commercial crop in Guatemala. Production was well established on the Pacific coast by the mid-1950s and increased steadily through the mid-1960s. Acreage and yields almost doubled in the 1962/63 crop year, which is about the time Miguelenses began working in cotton. The cotton harvest falls in January and February, just as the coffee season is closing, so many men return from coffee work only to leave immediately for the cotton fields. Because cotton is grown in the open sun of the torrid coastal plain, only strong men and older boys do this work.

The Indians generally dislike coastal labor because of the poor working conditions, the losses they suffer when they abandon their farms for several months at a stretch, and the low pay. Accustomed to *tierra fria,* Indians suffer in the hot tropics. The heat of the coast (especially in the cotton zone) is debilitating, water is impure, and malaria common. Working conditions on cotton plantations are the worst of all, largely because of massive insecticide spraying. So intensively are these poisons used that coastal wildlife has been threatened and hundreds of workers fall ill every season, some fatally (Adams 1970:370-71, 375-76).

Leaving the municipio for several months, Indians also suffer agriculturally. They abandon their ripening corn fields to the limited mercy of thieves, pests, and the elements. Livestock is either sold or left in the care of neighbors—in the first case, the family suffers because it sells when the market is glutted and has to repurchase on its return when many others are also trying to buy stock; in the second case, neighbors get free temporary benefit of the animals. One farmer recalled collecting 6000 pounds of precious sheep manure during his neighbors' absence.

The Indians' wages, furthermore, are low and are being eroded by inflation. During the Ubico period, coffee pickers were paid 10 cents per *cajón* (the 100-pound box that harvesters fill). Although it is generally said that a cajón is the equivalent of one *jornal* (day's wages), this depends on the abundance of the harvest and the number of pickers in the worker's family. Often it takes more than one day's work to fill a cajón. After the fall of Ubico, the Ponce government raised the wage to 20 cents per cajón, though Miguelenses claim not all fincas complied, and in 1945 the revolutionary government again raised the legal rate to 80 cents per cajón. Merchants in San Pedro still remember that year fondly, because returning *jornaleros* (wage workers) brought much more money back into the highlands than ever before.

From 1945 to the present, a span of three decades, Miguelenses claim not to have received a single legally sanctioned raise, and some fincas still do not pay the 1945 rate. Juan Mariano Ramírez, a farmer from Subchal, has worked at various times on four different fincas since 1947. In 1947, he received a jornal of 80 cents, plus a ration of 20 pounds of corn a week for himself and his wife, and five pounds for each working child. Coffee, lime, and sometimes salt were also provided by the finca. Since that time only one finca has raised its jornal (to 94 cents) and two have cut back on rations. Juan Mariano also feels he rarely receives an honest day's pay for an honest day's work. Only one finca he is familiar with actually weighs the cajón when it is received from the picker. The others demand that it be overfilled and tote it up as 100 pounds received. An agronomist I know took a job on a finca in 1965 where this method of payment was practiced, and to check his suspicions had a filled box weighed. He found it to contain 120 pounds of beans, fully a fifth more than the jornalero was paid for.

While wages have remained stagnant, prices have risen sharply and this trend continues. Checking price fluctuations with both consumers and merchants, I found general agreement that prices of all basic consumer goods— tools, clothing, and food—have been steadily increasing since the end of the Depression. Hard statistics are unavailable because merchants do not keep long-term records, but many have been in the same trade for decades and have a good knowledge of prices. Since the Depression, tool prices have risen by as much as 45 percent.[2] When the homemade "pajama" costume was still in style, an Indian could outfit himself with sandals, hat, shirt, and pants for about one quetzal. Now, the hat alone costs that much, and a complete outfit costs a minimum of Q5. As Indians have become more dependent on purchased corn, corn prices have also gone up. San Pedro merchants say the price of coastal corn was around Q2 per *quintal* (hundredweight) in the 1930s and sold for Q2.50 per quintal in San Pedro. Wagley notes that in 1937 corn in the Huehuetenango market sold for 50 cents per quintal after the harvest, rising to Q2 per quintal just before the next harvest (1941:24n). The average price of corn in interior San Marcos is now about Q4 per quintal.

As a comparative case, Hinshaw, in his restudy of Panajachel, was able to make very accurate estimates of the general rise in Indian cost of living by comparing current expenditures with those recorded by Tax in 1936 (1975:16-22). Hinshaw found the overall increase in the cost of food staples to be 370 percent, and clothing, 300 percent.

Wage labor on coastal plantations allows the Indians of San Miguel to survive despite their agrarian problems. By migrating seasonally to the fincas they have maintained their highlands existence and much of their traditional culture. But this adaptation is a meager one that is reducing the level and quality of their lives. The double-edged trap of stagnant wages and rising prices results from the powerlessness of seasonal workers, the most disorganized and defenseless sector of Guatemala's laboring class. As inflation worsens and the Indian population continues to grow, the laborers' position can only continue to degenerate. In San Miguel the bottom is being reached. At present, the only Miguelenses who make a decent living from coffee—Guatemala's principal product—are the habilitadores, who invariably have more possessions, newer clothes, better quarters, and larger farms than anyone else in the township.

Summary

The people of San Miguel no longer have sufficient land to support themselves with agriculture or to maintain an autonomous agrarian adaptation. As farm production has declined, the Miguelenses have been left with one major resource, their labor, which they relinquish on the worst terms. These Indians are no longer peasants; their economic situation exhibits all the classic characteristics of a rural seasonal proletariat:

1. The means of production owned by the group, namely land, has diminished in output.
2. The people have been pushed deeply into a plantation labor market.
3. Money earned in this market does not circulate within the community, but is rapidly spent on necessities to the benefit of outside merchants.
4. The only community members who are progressing to any degree are engaged in illegal activities (the contrabandistas) or are agents of their own people's exploitation (the habilitadores).
5. The community lacks the power to demand improvements in its situation.

Notes

[1] A *cuerda* is a unit of land area commonly used in Guatemala. Its dimensions vary from locale to locale, but in highland San Marcos it is approximately 4727 feet square (.04 hectare or .11 acre).

[2] In the early 1940s hoes ranged in price from Q1 to Q1.75, depending on size. The same hoes

now range from Q1.75 to Q3.25. A mattock cost Q1 then, and now sells for Q1.75. Sickles have gone up from Q.25 to Q.40 and were recently raised to Q.85 by a new import tax. Five-pound axe-heads that cost Q2.50 five years ago are now up to Q4, and Indians complain that they are of poorer quality.

EIGHT

Social Change in San Miguel

As its involvement in the cash sector grew, San Miguel's social organization underwent important modifications. Over the last three or four decades intrusive political and religious organizations have reduced the municipio's autonomy and internal homogeneity. Once again we see that beneath the outward appearances of cultural stability, important features of life in this township have changed markedly in recent years. The prerequisites and organization of community power have been altered, new religious ideologies have been introduced, and consequently the number of groups within community society has increased. All these changes have affected San Miguel's fiesta system.

Changes in Political Organization

Before the changes wrought by the Ubico period and the subsequent revolution, the formal political organization of the community conformed to the standard highland-Indian type (Adams 1957; Bunzel 1967; Nash 1958; Wagley 1949). The primary political figures were the prestigious elders (*principales*), the mayors, and the head chimán, who in San Miguel was called the *Cabeza del Pueblo* (head of the community). A man became an elder by donating much of his life to public service and by proving to his fellow citizens that he was a worthy leader. The qualifications of leadership were decision-making talent, forcefulness, and speaking ability. In describing the old principales, people would say, "they were the ones who had laws in their heads," or, "it was they who spoke for everyone." Even a poor man, it is said, could become a *principal* if he had these talents and used them to earn the respect of the people.

The principales were instrumental in selecting the alcaldes, cofrades, and other municipal officials. The formal administration was headed by two alcaldes, a first and a second, the second serving as vice mayor, much as the first *regidor* (councilman) does today. Assisting the mayor were a municipal council, auxiliary officials in the aldeas, and a number of young men who had policing and maintenance duties. Young men began their public careers in these menial posts and worked their way up according to their capabilities. Interspersed with political posts were ceremonial offices in which men were expected to serve. Informants refer to these posts as cargos, and both political and religious officials had important ceremonial duties. Officials were selected in yearly meetings of principales and outgoing municipal and aldean officials. In open discussion potential candidates were reviewed, selections made, and appointments ceremonially ratified by the head chimán. Runners notified the appointees, whose acceptance was virtually obligatory.

This system of centralized, gerontocratic, appointive administration was changed by fiat when Ubico took power and replaced indigenous mayors with his own intendentes. During this period the municipio came under more direct external control, which was exerted primarily to exploit Indian labor for plantation work and road-building.

National government again changed character with the 1944 Revolution, when the autocratic, centralized administration of the dictator was replaced by a liberal regime interested in protecting the Indians and incorporating them into national life. The revolutionary governments of Arévalo and Arbenz decreed that local politics would be electoral, and encouraged the founding of political parties and other interest groups at the grass-roots level. In San Miguel, these innovations changed local politics totally and permanently. Power is now based on party organization and external political affiliation, rather than on social standing derived from service and charisma. Elderly men and shamans enjoy no special political prerogatives, civil officers are selected by popular vote instead of by appointment, and the separation of political from ritual organization which began under the intendentes has been made even more formal and complete. Adams describes similar post-Revolution political changes in other Guatemalan municipios (1957).

Along with the structural changes of the post-Revolution period came a growing political awareness on the part of individuals. Miguelenses are by no means politically well informed, but they are now much more active in their own behalf than they were previously. Virtually all Miguelense men and many women can now converse in Spanish, which has given them greater courage to deal with outsiders. Radios, scarce as they are, have also reduced Miguelense ignorance about the outside world. The Indians have been encouraged by some governments to work politically for themselves, and they now are more knowledgeable about the law, lawyers, and bureaucrats. There were two viable political parties in the township, and during the election year of 1970 a third, the Christian Democrats, successfully established a local organization and ran a slate of candidates for municipal office. When the Christian Democratic candidate for president spoke in a neighboring municipio, a group of Miguelenses hiked over to hear him, evidence of their growing political interest.

A political demonstration that took place in San Miguel in the early 1950s is indicative of Indians' political capabilities. After the Revolution of 1944, some Indians in San Miguel organized a local agency of the revolutionary party then in national power. One of the founders and long-time treasurer of the party was Chepe Aguilar of Subchal. Chepe, who subsequently played a significant role in the ceremonial reorganization of his aldea, is a unique and extraordinary individual. He was born into a poor family, and his youth was so occupied in helping his father support the family that he received no formal education. But, as he says, *yo tengo buena inteligencia* (I am very smart) and his intelligence has served him well. He is a carpenter and mason of real skill, he has installed certain improvements in his own home—glass windows that can be opened, and a cleverly hung door—that I have seen nowhere else in the community. He can make pottery and bake bread. He learned to tailor by observing craftsmen in Tejutla and now supports himself with his craft, at which he is both expert and innovative. He speaks rapidly and emphatically in a jackhammar stacatto of Mam and Spanish that clearly bends others to his will. He has been discussed as a candidate for municipal mayor, and the parish priest says Chepe is his most advanced catechist, even though he neither reads nor writes. By his forcefulness, his intelligence, and his accomplishments, Chepe is a natural leader.

The most significant action that Chepe's party took during its brief existence led to its suppression and demise. In the early 1950s, Indian memories of Ubico's opression were still intense, even more so than today because only a decade had passed since they had been "liberated" from the labor laws of that period. Consequently, when the municipal officials attempted to impress free labor for the construction of the Tejutla-San Miguel road, Indians were provoked to act. The despised *vialidad*, the highway construction corvée of the Ubico period, seemed to be reemerging. "They even wanted us to supply our own tools," Chepe complained, "like they do in Cuba."

A demonstration was to occur in the cabecera, and the revolutionary party apparently had some role in its organization. The results were tragic. The Indians were on their own ground and angry, so angry that the Ladinos in the cabecera feared for their own safety. Violence of unspecified origin began; a squad of three nervous soldiers, there to maintain order, fired into the crowd, killing one Indian and wounding two others. A larger detachment of soldiers subsequently arrived from the Quezaltenango barracks, arresting 60 men and thus suppressing the "revolt."

The soldiers also hunted down and arrested leaders of the party. Chepe, who was not present at the demonstration, spent 20 days hiding in the forest near Tutuapa, and finally surrendered himself to the authorities in Ixtahuacán to put an end to the harassment of his wife and daughter by army patrols. During the emergency the municipio was being administered by an *interventor*, a Ladino from Tejutla, who had to decide Chepe's case locally since the Quezaltenango jail was already full. Chepe pleaded that there was nothing illegal about party politics and that he had not been present at the demonstration. The interventor sentenced him to 30 days in jail in lieu of a Q200 fine that Chepe could not possibly have paid. After four days in jail he made a plea for penalty reduction and was let off with a Q50 fine. To raise the money Chepe was forced to sell a parcel of land and his carpentry tools, and to borrow Q15 from a schoolteacher.

Chepe is still not sure what his crime was, but he is convinced that politics is a prohibitive game (especially when national regimes change), and he now adamantly refuses to involve himself in any political action beyond casting his vote. For the community, the demonstration was a clumsy attempt to exert pressure, and considering the loss of life and subsequent suppression of one of their fledgling political agencies, it was counterproductive. The demonstration nevertheless gave evidence of a certain degree of new-found political energy. For the first time, Miguelenses had spoken out for themselves.

Another significant political development is that *progress* is now a central concept in the political rhetoric of San Miguel. Municipal administrations are dedicated to improving health facilities and schools. Since the mayorship is now electoral and since there is more than one party, candidates must campaign, and their campaigns are based on progressive promises. Politicians both in and out of office are also fond of boasting of their role in bringing new resources to the township. Recent municipal administrations can boast a number of accomplishments. There are schools in all aldeas now, and virtually all the young people are conversant in Spanish. There is a road connecting San Miguel with the outside world. Vehicles enter and leave daily. One can now travel to Guatemala City in a single day, whereas just a few years ago it took longer than that to reach San Marcos. The roofed areas in the El Triunfo and cabecera markets have been greatly increased. As I left the field, yet another school was being constructed in aldea El Salitre, a conduit was being laid for a potable water system in the cabecera, and San Miguel was competing with neighboring municipios for the route of a proposed new road to Huehuetenango. These projects and accomplishments indicate a level of public ambition that was absent before the 1944 Revolution.

Politically, then, the municipio has changed in small but significant ways, beginning with the Ubico regime. The basis of power has been altered, modern forms of political participation have developed, internal political diversification has taken place, and people have increased their political knowledge and spirit. Similar trends have taken place in religion, in that local syncretic institutions have given ground to crusading international churches. Here, too, the personnel, autonomy, and power of the indigenous system have been significantly altered.

Changes in Religious Organization

The job of the missionaries, who began arriving in the community in the 1950s, was not one of awakening religious spirit in a previously secular region, since highland Indians are profoundly spiritual people. Instead, the missionaries' task was to reform this religiousness according to their own doctrines. There were serious obstacles to be overcome. The people were sincere adherents of folk Catholicism, and the chimanes, especially, had important interests in the native religion, which they protected with all the authority at their command.

Both Protestantism and Catholicism have won converts and established solid grass-roots organizations in San Miguel, though Catholicism presently holds an edge. The present priest counts 280 families that he considers faithful parishioners because they have been formally married or remarried in the Church and are in regular attendance. Protestants boast of at most half that number, the majority of whom are concentrated in the cabecera and aldeas Sícabe and La Patria. Protestantism is growing among the Miguelenses, however, and is a prominent aspect of the current social scene. The municipal mayor who was elected during my stay is a Protestant. Members of his faith have recently constructed a church in the cabecera and a chapel in aldea El Triunfo.

Espiritismo, another religious movement of growing popularity in the entire San Marcos region, is practiced in San Miguel by a small number of people who are secretive about their involvement. More a system of occult belief than a religion, espiritismo seems related to Western spiritualism, with heavier emphasis on spiritual healing.

In contrast to its earlier uniformity, then, the municipio is now divided into four ideologies: folk Catholicism, orthodox Catholicism, Protestantism, and spiritualism. Indians participate in all these religions, Ladinos only in orthodox Catholicism and Protestantism.

The first latter-day Catholic missionary to work in the municipio was Padre Cipriano Gómez, who arrived in the late 1950s. Padre Cipriano, a Spaniard, was a man of incredible energy who left his mark on the townships of San Lorenzo, Sipacapa, Concepción, and Tejutla, as well as on San Miguel. Everyone in the region remembers him with strong emotion. Old Ladinas display his photograph on their walls; Indian converts speak of him with reverence; and a contemporary priest credits him with "reawakening the Catholic spirit in the entire region." Chimanes also remember him by repeatedly destroying shrines erected at the place where, in the early 1960s, he was killed in an auto accident.

At the beginning of his short career, Pade Cipriano adopted the emerging national strategy for Indian missionization: the training of catechist missionaries in *cursillos* (indoctrination courses). He began by searching out those few men who seemed most amenable to orthodox conversion, those who were, for some reason, skeptical of the native religion. These men were trained in Catholic doctrine by the padre, then sent to proselytize in their aldeas. This program of group instruction to produce lay missionaries has grown stronger over the years. The local cursillos given by pioneering priests such as Padre Cipriano have been expanded to the departmental and national levels. San Miguel catequistas now attend advanced courses in Tejutla and San Marcos, and some have studied in Guatemala City.

The advantages of employing catequistas as missionaries are numerous. The mountains are so rugged that even Indians exhaust themselves in their daily activities. A priest working alone could not effectively deal with a single interior municipio, and Padre Cipriano worked in several. Through the catequistas he greatly extended his coverage and increased its efficiency. This was especially true since native catequistas naturally know their aldeas more intimately than an immigrant Spaniard ever could. They were thus more familiar with potential converts and could approach them more effectively. The program also intensified the religious experience of the converts, whose missionary work forced them to actively study and live their new religion.

The missionaries introduced new ideologies to San Miguel. More important, they established new social groupings to assist missionization and church administration. These new groups represent an elaboration and diversification of the community social structure. They present individuals with open, secure alternatives to traditional forms of association. The new Catholic society is intricately organized. The priests have established a set of central committees through which parishioners, both Indian and Ladino, are given responsibility for church maintenance, improvements, and finances. The aldeas have similar organizations for maintaining their chapels, and so on. The Catholics of each aldea are led by a "senior brother," who officiates at meetings, and a "first catechist," who leads prayers in the absence of the priest. A number of religiously trained "designates" are responsible for the missionary effort. Below these officials, the rest of the community is divided into *pagadores* (dues-paying adults) and *almas* (other converts).

These organizations have provided an entirely new arena for prestige competition. Converts often discuss one another in terms of the number of cursillos each has attended and their respective knowledge of Catholic doctrine. The titles and roles of senior brother and first catechist carry authority and respect. Competition between convert groups in different aldeas is also keen. Aldean groups vie with one another in building and improving chapels. Two aldeas purchased bells for their chapels during my stay, and chapel-building elsewhere is proceeding at (locally speaking) a brisk pace.

The new groups are also highly supportive and open to new members. This was demonstrated in a rosary service held for a newly married couple in Subchal. The service was held by the father of the bride, on the night of the wedding. So many people attended that his house could not have held another person. Bernardo López, a "designate," led the prayer after waiting over an hour for the "first catechist," who did not show up. The first catechist, interestingly, is a more recent convert than Bernardo, but has been to more cursillos. Bernardo's deference in respectfully waiting for his arrival indicates that accomplishment is of primary importance to advancement in the new broherhood.

The rosary included the usual sequence of prayers, interrupted by a long sermon drawn from Paul's letter to the Corinthians. Bernardo emphasized the passage on sexual fidelity in marriage, for the benefit of the young couple, and elaborated his topic with surprising skill. Several business matters were considered after the service, one of them concerning a recent convert who had been ill for several months. Volunteers were organized to work his land and a collection was taken up to buy him medicines. Afterward, the meeting became a purely social affair.

The religious societies are new segments of community structure complete with ideologies, rules for joining, opportunities for social advancement, a spirit of common welfare, and considerable cohesion. Their appearance and success are related to a number of events. Protestant missionaries were invited to work in Guatemala in 1882 by Justo Rufino Barrios, though they did not begin serious work in San Miguel until the 1960s. After the 1944 Revolution, the government relaxed its control of the Catholic Church, opening Guatemala's doors to Catholic missionization for the first time since the suppression of the Church by Barrios in the nineteenth century. Many of these newcomers took up work in mountain parishes such as San Miguel, which had had no resident priest for decades. Both Catholic and Protestant missionaries have made strong efforts to reach even the most isolated groups, and on a national scale both have actively promoted schools, cooperatives, and other social welfare programs.

In San Miguel, Catholic medical clinics have also played a critical role in mission success, for faith and healing are intimately entwined in the Indian mind. Padre Cipriano introduced San Miguel to modern medicine, bringing in various drugs and preventive medicines that he distributed through the catechists whom he trained to give injections. The man reported to be the first convert in the municipio recounts that he was initially attracted to Catholicism because Padre Cipriano cured him of malaria. He had contracted the disease six years earlier on the fincas, and paid the chimanes Q60 for treatments that were "without effect."

Effects

National institutions have penetrated San Miguel, moderating its political autonomy and social isolation, and stamping it with the indelible beginnings of diversification. Being Catholic in San Miguel is radically different from being *de costumbre* or Protestant. Each association prescribes certain social rules for its adherents, along with a distinctive set of rituals and a particular relationship between man and God, and in so doing each defines a distinct subgroup with many unique customs. Political involvement is no longer traditional, as there are now competing bases of power and new alignments with outside sources of power and resources. Political motivations have shifted from complete emphasis on internal order and group protection through isolation, to a cautious interst in probing the outside world for what it might offer.

These alterations may appear minor, but we should not underestimate their impact on people's lives. Contemporary Miguelenses are faced with options and possibilities that their ancestors could not have imagined. They have begun to experience the crisis of choice, which affects their daily lives at all levels. Old men lament the passing of tradition and lash out at the *evangélicos* and other conspirators against the ancient ways. Younger men are caught in spiritual dilemmas, wrestling with the pros and cons of the available religions. Their considerations are complex: a man recently converted to Catholicism said he had considered the expensive rituals required in the folk religion and wondered if they were worth it, since the priests were teaching that "they were not valid before the Lord, and were a waste of money." Besides, he said, the chimanes were on the wane, and what if his sons grew up in the folk religion and there were no experts to assist them in the complicated costumbres? Had the traditional morality been intact and unthreatened, this man would never have been troubled by such thoughts. Even in the cultural backwater of San Miguel, the complexities of modern life have made their initial appearance and worked their inevitable influence on native devotion to native ways.

The socioeconomic changes described in these last two chapters provide the backdrop against which breakdown in the fiesta system of San Miguel must be understood. Ceremonial change in this municipio stems from agrarian failure, which has increased the felt costs of religious giving. As these costs grew, furthermore, incorporation of the community into national political and religious institutions weakened the pressures and rewards underlying fiesta sponsorhip. Municipal politics have been secularized, even conservative mayors find it difficult to force people into religious office, and prestige can be earned in new ways. This process is evaluated and analyzed in chapter 11. Now we shall turn our attention to San Pedro, where accelerating development provides an instructive counterpoint to the community just described.

NINE

San Pedro:
A Developing Indian Town

In the last three decades the Indian town of San Pedro has become powerful, dynamic, and progressive. Anthropologists refer to such development in community culture as modernization; San Pedranos call it *civilización*. Both terms denote the pervasive change whereby a community suddenly becomes economically, socially, and culturally mobile, forsaking its previously enclosed condition in a transformation as dramatic as birth. In San Miguel Ixtahuacán a few men have become wealthy enough to improve the conditions of their families, but such progress is occasional and adventitious. In San Pedro it has become a community process. Ceremonial reorganization has been one aspect of the civilizing process in this town. As the community has modernized, its fiesta system has come to resemble that of the dominant national classes, with only vestiges of ancient rites remaining.

This chapter outlines the recent development of San Pedro, describing the principal changes that have occurred over the last generation, their interrelationships and causes. The population of this municipio is organized into a cabecera and 17 hamlets scattered about the hinterland. The cabecera is a very large town by rural Guatemalan standards, having a population of about 10,000; the aldeas are much smaller, with a combined population of some 15,000. Cultural development has progressed much further in the town than in the hamlets, and the following discussion, except where indicated, focuses on the town.

Economic Change

San Pedro is unique among Indian communities of highland San Marcos, for it alone has advanced into a competitive position in the national economy.

Compared to other populations in the area, San Pedranos hold more skills, broader knowledge, and better productive capital; as a result they are attached to the nation by an intricate network of profitable commercial relations rather than by the trap of seasonal finca labor. The town is alive with energy: the main streets are lined with Indian-owned shops and warehouses selling consumer goods and raw materials for various small industries; even late at night looms slam, sewing machines chatter, and diesel trucks pull in and out. In the years I lived in this town I saw its economic pace slacken only once. During a nighttime power failure, work came to a forced halt and people chatted and strummed guitars by candlelight, like residents of some sleepy Indian village.

Economic takeoff in San Pedro has occurred since World War II. Before the war, Indians were peasant producers whose commerce was largely confined to the regional market. The people were naturales, by their own definition. The first generation of Spanish-speaking youngsters was just maturing, and most of the traditional ceremonies were still observed. Few San Pedranos had completed secondary education. Housing, dress, and other forms of consumption were predominantly Indian.

Until around 1950 the progressive sector of the local economy was in the hands of a few immigrant families. Being the center of regional trade, San Pedro attracted immigrant entrepreneurs. Early in the century foreign families began trickling in—a Chinese, a Lebanese, a Mexican, a German, and several Italians. They set up stores, and prospered by supplying the region with industrial goods. Highland San Marcos was at this time an isolated region, but one with a demand for hardware, textiles, and other foreign industrial goods. It was also a region that produced a small surplus of wheat, wool, and handwoven textiles, which were valuable in the external market. These sophisticated immigrants provided the connection between local and external economy. Most of them established *almacenes* (general stores) selling tools, wearing apparel, and processed foodstuffs. Many were also buyers of local surplus goods, and one family ran a small bank.

All of the immigrants are now gone, except for a few of the old fathers who have retired in San Pedro, and a woman of German descent who owns a grocery store. In almost every instance the commercial wealth of the fathers financed the education of their sons, who are now professionals in Guatemala City. Many sons of these immigrant families are quite prominent: one is an internationally known cancer specialist, another is head of the Instituto Nutricional de Centro América y Panamá. Still another owns various large enterprises, including an enormous coffee finca, and is reputed to be one of the wealthiest men in Guatemala.

The immigrants remained aloof from the Indians. Relations were largely cordial, but the two groups did not intermarry, and the immigrants sent their children away to the better schools of Guatemala City. Interaction between the two groups was principally economic. Indians were customers of the immigrants, and with their mules transported the immigrants' wares from Quezaltenango and the Pacific Coast to San Pedro.

The Indian sector of the economy was based on agriculture, mule trade, and a variety of cottage industries. In the township, San Pedranos grew standard subsistence crops, and some wealthier Indians owned coastal plots where they raised cattle or produced corn, rice, and tropical fruits.

San Pedro has traditionally been the major trade center in the department, and San Pedranos have always been the principal traders. The Thursday plaza has been the largest in the department for as long as people can remember. Before the introduction of trucks, many San Pedranos drove their mule trains along weekly trade routes between their town and the plazas of Quezaltenango, the interior, or the coast.

Much of the population worked in handicrafts, usually in combination with subsistence agriculture. So important have crafts been in the town's economy that in 1929 the government founded a local industrial institute to encourage and elaborate Indian skills. Brickmaking, construction, baking, and the production of cloth, clothing, leather, and shoes were traditional San Pedro industries. Handwoven textiles were a major product, and, along with other handicraft goods, were produced almost exclusively for the local market. O'Neale visted San Pedro in 1936 during her field study of Indian textile arts. She refers to the town as a "flourishing textile center," producing cotton and silk skirts, brocaded *huipiles* (traditional blouses), table coverings, and pillow tops. Simple tailoring was also important, and she noticed an "unusual number" of shirts, such as those worn by men of surrounding municipios, for sale in the market. She makes no mention, though, of textile production for national or international markets (O'Neale 1945).

There was marked social stratification in San Pedro even before the recent economic expansion. Immigrant entrepreneurs, who owned the most profitable businesses, were the top elite. The Indians were economically inferior and culturally distinct from the immigrants, and were themselves stratified—much more so than the populations of the surrounding Indian municipios. With its richer and more central economy, San Pedro contained a

group of well-to-do Indians who owned large flocks, extensive coastal holdings, and long strings of mules.

Even before development, then, San Pedro was a unique and, in many
ways, a favored Indian town. It had a much larger, more concentrated
population than most Indian communities, an intrusive foreign elite, a complex and rich economy, and unusual social differentiation. Tax visited the
community in the 1930s and was impressed by its uniqueness. He was
particularly intrigued by the women weavers, about whom he made this
cryptic statement:

> I cannot explain the exceptional case of the women of San Pedro
> Sacatepéquez (Department of San Marcos), where Indian women work
> at foot looms in the shops. This is an extraordinary town, the only one I
> know that is a Spanish-type town in every respect except that it is
> populated exclusively by Indians. Perhaps if one studied the place he
> would discover that in some sense all of the Indians have become
> Ladinoized; and that might explain the anomaly of the women foot-
> loom operators (1953:26n).

Over the last few decades a large number of successful entrepreneurs
have emerged in several sectors of the San Pedro economy. Most of the old
mule traders have been replaced by truckers, and commercial establishments
formerly owned by foreigners have been purchased by Indian businessmen.
Some of these merchants have capital investments in excess of Q30,000.
Anselmo Orozco, a trucker, is one of the most successful entrepreneurs. The
approximate value of his major holdings in 1969 were:

Q10,000	10-ton GMC diesel truck
3,000	2-ton Toyota pickup truck
18,000	house, warehouse, and property in downtown San Pedro
3,000	agricultural land
Q34,000	TOTAL

There is some indebtedness on the trucks, but he owns the real estate outright.
He owns as well as a large inventory of soap, cement, flour, and bulk cooking
oil, and has cash savings of at least several thousand quetzals.

Indian students from San Pedro have trained themselves for careers in
education, law, agricultural science, the military, engineering, and, in one
case to date, medicine. A recent monograph on San Pedro written by a native
schoolteacher contains a roster of 72 native professionals, not including
schoolteachers who were "too numerous to mention" (Consuegra n.d.:45-

46). Some of these students have moved to Guatemala City or other places around the country; many have returned to work in their home municipio. The textile arts have flourished beyond what O'Neale might have imagined in her most radical speculations. Native handwoven cloth is now produced for an international market and the weaving industry continues to absorb labor. Tailors have honed their skills to such a degree that the fine apparel they make is now sold in the best shops of Quezaltenango and Guatemala City. A completely new machine-knitting industry has sprung up since the mid-1950s; two men have already established small factories with electric machines. Guatemala is truly a land of contrasts; on the very rim of the depressed and primitive interior, San Pedro's economy is booming.

Agriculture lags far behind commerce, education, and the textile industry as a factor in local development. This is in the common highland pattern: where Indian communities are enjoying real economic advance, this advance has been principally mercantile and educational. Farming around San Pedro has moved little beyond its traditional state. There has been some expansion of wheat production and truck farming, but corn and beans grown for subsistence are still the principal crops, and farmers have done little in the way of experimentation or in adopting new technology. Agriculture in the valley of San Pedro is nevertheless more productive than in the slash-and-burn zones; soil is more fertile, land more abundant, and subsistence more secure. Occasionally a campesino from aldeas such as Chamac or Champollop will do coast work in his slack season, hiring himself out with his mules to bring in a coastal farmer's corn crop. No one from these communities, however, contracts himself to the fincas. Their own farms fill most of their needs, so San Pedrano campesinos do wage work only as an occasional means of earning spare cash.

This pattern of economic progress, strong in one sector and weak in another, corresponds to the post-war investment opportunities that have developed in the highlands. Road building has brought a new measure of economic integration to the region, which has been especially profitable to crossroads communities such as San Pedro. Expansion of the school system, another government priority in recent decades, has also benefited people living in and around urban zones, where most of these facilities are located. Farmers, on the other hand, have received no such stimulation. The Guatemalan government has yet to commit itself to the costly program of agricultural planning, research, extension agencies, credit, and price support that is necessary to upgrade highland agriculture.

Compared to agrarian development, commercial development is a simple affair. When new roads made trucking feasible, General Motors, Ford, Thames, and other firms opened agencies in Guatemala City, providing sales, service, and financing for their vehicles. Coming from a community with a long commercial tradition, men from San Pedro were naturally inclined to exchange their mules for faster, more capacious conveyances as the opportunity presented itself.

Perhaps the most dramatic example of commercial entrepreneurship in San Pedro is that of the Orozco brothers. German and Anselmo Orozco were born in Chamac, sons of a peasant farmer and brickmaker. Their parents are naturales who live in one of the poorer houses in the aldea. German, the elder brother, completed primary school and labored in his father's brickworks until he was shanghaied into the Guatemalan army at age 18. Though his father wanted him released as essential household labor, German had ideas of seeing the world and refused to cooperate.

German learned to drive trucks and motorcyles in the army and was favored by a colonel, also a San Pedrano, who appreciated his intelligence and impressive appearance. After military service in the capital, German could not bring himself to return to the brickworks, even though he had hereditary rights to mine clay from the communal field. He found his father's work "very heavy," so with the aid of his colonel he found employment as a motorcycle officer in the National Police force. For the next 15 years he lived and worked in Guatemala City.

Anselmo had meanwhile completed two years of school, done a brief unhappy stint in the army, and returned to Chamac to settle with an Indian wife. Landless and poor, he moved into a small hut and set up shop as a soapmaker. Every week he purchased tallow in large drums, collected ashes from his neighbors' kitchens, and made soap to sell in the weekend coastal plazas. To aid in ash collection, he purchased a decrepit one-eyed horse—the first means of transport owned by the man who is now one of the wealthiest truckers in the region.

Anselmo and his wife ate simply, dressed simply, and worked hard; their goal was to save, not to live ostentatiously. Each week they processed 400 pounds of tallow into soap and each weekend Anselmo hitched a ride to the coast on a friend's truck and sold the whole batch. Later, while visiting his brother in the capital, he discovered an outlet where he could purchase tallow at half price, and his profits immediately increased.

Anselmo realized that the soap business was a dead end. Since it was handicraft work, there was no way he could expand production, and he was beginning to face stiff competition from new industrial soaps. He had seen firsthand, however, the value of vehicles. With a truck one had great mobility and could buy bulk goods wherever they were cheapest, and sell them in small quantities where they were scarce. Profits were not limited as in handicraft labor. San Pedro was full of small industries needing raw materials and small traders needing transport. The San Pedro-San Marcos urban area itself constituted a large, growing market for industrial goods, and Anselmo knew many local men who were doing very well with trucks. He conferred with German and they pooled their savings to purchase a used 4-ton truck.

The brothers have prospered as truckers. At present, each owns a 10-ton diesel, a pickup truck for local deliveries, and a house and warehouse in downtown San Pedro from which they run their wholesale businesses. Their children will all receive higher education, and each brother has one son about to graduate from the local military academy. In two generations this aldean family has become wealthy and modern.

Trucking and commerce. I could not discover exactly when San Pedranos began to purchase trucks, but most entered the business after World War II. Informants recalled that although there were vehicles in the region in the 1940s, the business took off in the 1950s. A survey showed that at least 26 San Pedranos had tried the trucking business by 1960, some successfully, some not. San Marcos Ladinos were the first in the region to purchase vehicles, a few having owned them before the war. The local transport industry, in fact, had its beginnings among the more cosmopolitan Marquenses, but the Ladinos were subsequently driven out of business by the emerging San Pedro *transportistas*. Now there are more luxury automobiles in San Marcos than in San Pedro, but many more work vehicles in San Pedro. In 1970 I counted 42 trucks of 8-ton capacity or more, owned by 30 San Pedranos. Almost all these men entered the business in the 1960s and most are both freight-haulers and merchants. Trucking is still a growing business, though old hands are beginning to complain of competition. "One used to be able to make real money with a truck," one said, "but now the streets are paved with them."

Most successful truckers go through a similar pattern of development. Beginning with small savings, they purchase a used truck to haul freight. If owners are shrewd and hard-working, they can move up to a small diesel in a year or so, and purchase successively larger vehicles as their savings grow. Some men have several large trucks and employ their sons as drivers. Among the diligent ones, income is not only sufficient to finance vehicles of increasing size and quality, but eventually to open *bodegas* (warehouses) to sell various kinds of merchandise.[1]

In addition to bodegas, San Pedrano merchants sell goods in the town plaza, in the *mercado,* and in stores of varying sizes. The mercado is an enclosed structure covering a large block, divided into numerous permanent stalls. The plaza, adjacent to the mercado, is the site of open-air selling every day that weather permits. Stores range from small corner groceries and cantinas carrying around Q50 in stock to large almacenes selling hardware, food, and dry goods. The former are notable only in their great number. A lawyer in Guatemala City, son of one of the Italian immigrant entrepreneurs, told me that he hardly recognizes his home town anymore; almost every house has a store in it. This is not an exaggeration, since there are virtually no simple dwellings in San Pedro. Almost all houses are also stores, workshops, or bodegas.

People say that the commercial development of San Pedro's main streets is a recent thing. Previously, the streets were less *alegre* (active), being lined with houses and the occasional shops and stores of immigrant merchants. Surveying the 25 major commercial establishments in the central district, I found that 24 of them were set up in their present location during the 1960s, although many of these had been in business elsewhere for years before moving to the central zone. Of these establishments, the oldest is an almacén established around 1945.

The town's major commercial zone lies along two one-way streets that form the principal routes through town. On these nine city blocks a broad range of goods and services is preently available: suits, sweaters, and shoes (locally made or imported), hardware, paint, dry goods, construction materials, and food both wholesale and retail. One can also buy fresh meat and fresh bread, see either of two doctors, and have watches and radios repaired. Except for one doctor and the German grocer, the proprietors of all these establishments are local Indians.

Textiles. The textile industry (weaving, tailoring, knitting) has also grown in size, increased the quality and number of its products, and attained a higher degree of organization over the last three decades. Though still primarily a handicraft industry, it now employs more people, uses improved materials and equipment, and produces for national and international markets.

Since there is no new capital to amplify output per worker, the weaving industry has had to grow by attracting labor.[2] Production is organized by a small number of Indian textile merchants who supply capital and market products. Each *patrón,* as these merchants are called, makes regular trips to Guatemala City, where he purchases yarn and delivers finished textiles to tourist shops and exporters. On his return, the patrón distributes the yarn to his weavers, who work in their homes, and tells them what kinds of cloth to produce. When they finish he pays them for their work, discounting the value of the yarn, and leaves again for Guatemala City. What has emerged in the weaving business (and in tailoring and knitting businesses as well) is an incipient form of the *putting-out* firm common in industrializing England (Smelser 1959). The patrons are true capitalists since they provide raw materials, direct work, and sell the product. Often they will finance the purchase of looms for their wevers, although they usually do not own the looms themselves. Some patrons have up to 100 weavers working for them. They are a new managerial elite that has become increasingly wealthy and powerful in recent years.

Weavers themselves profit less than the patrons from this expanding industry, since they are caught in a labor trap, much as Anselmo was in the soap business. The weavers' output is limited by their physical energy; there is no labor-saving technology to help them expand. Given the limitations of the manual loom, weavers can earn about Q.75 per day. Working six days a week for 50 weeks of the year yields a maximum yearly income of Q225 (weavers almost invariably devote some time to subsistence farming). Patrons, on the other hand, are not so limited. Reinvesting profits to patronize more weavers, they continually expand their businesses. Many San Pedranos are so successful that they have diversified into trucking, retailing, and farming.

Despite the upper limit on income, weaving is an attractive occupation to many San Pedranos—so much so that farmers now complain about the difficulty of finding part-time field help. Weaving diversifies family operations and makes income more secure. Cash income from weaving is steady and subject to few risks. The work is indoors, so it is more pleasant than agriculture, especially during the rainy season. Women and youngsters can weave, contributing cash to family income, an important factor in an expanding consumer economy.

The tailoring industry has been stimulated by new skills as well as by an expanding market. These skills have been introduced over the last several decades by a few men who had the foresight to take correspondence courses in tailoring techniques, and the skills have spread through the community via a vigorous apprenticeship system. Master tailors have trained numerous highly proficient apprentices, as have master weavers and master knitters. The vigor of the apprenticeship system is a clear indicator of the health of San Pedro textile industries. Established operators are not afraid to train competitors in a rapidly expanding market.

The history of the knitting industry largely recapitulates that of the other two, except that here new material capital was a primary stimulator of growth. Knitting machines first became available in San Pedro in the mid-1950s and the number of operators has since grown steadily. As with weaving and tailoring, the art is taught through apprenticeship and in the local industrial institute. Knitting is done largely by women, while tailoring and weaving are primarily men's occupations.

Education. Education, the third important area of local development, was the first route to mobility exploited by San Pedranos. Early in this century a few of the people who managed to earn teaching degrees returned to work in San Pedro. After World War II, professional degrees became increasingly easy to obtain as secondary schools were established in San Marcos and, more recently, in San Pedro. The first public normal school was opened in San Marcos in the mid-1940s and has since been joined by a private secondary school, a Catholic *colegio,* and a military academy. All of these schools have had strong contingents of San Pedrano students ever since they were founded. Over 50 percent of the enrollment at the normal school now comes from San Pedro. San Pedro itself has a trade school and numerous primary schools. In the early 1960s, groups of San Pedro schoolteachers organized two night schools to enable working people to conveniently pursue secondary education.

New Sources of Prestige

The Indians of San Pedro have grown progressively wealthier in the post-war decades as they have exploited these new investment opportunities. Some have profited much more than others, but San Pedranos in general are remarkably prosperous. This prosperity has generated an impressive consumer economy, as the growing numbers of retail establishments indicate. San Pedranos now spend considerably more on housing, furnishings, and clothing than they did previously, and spend much more than do the people of surrounding townships, with the possible exception of San Marcos. They are growing more and more discontented with dirt floors, outhouses, open fires, and unglazed windows. New brick houses with tile floors and indoor plumbing are springing up all over town and are beginning to appear in nearby hamlets. Modern furniture and clothing are fashionable. Young people, especially students studying in San Marcos or Guatemala City, are important in changing consumption patterns, since they live according to the styles of their new reference group. During school vacations, the public square in San Pedro is a fascinating melange of traditional Indian costumes and miniskirts. As retailers have grown more confident of the public's ability to pay and wholesalers more confident of retailers' ability to sell, the consumer economy has been further stimulated by credit selling. All major consumer goods (radios, phonographs, applicances, bicycles) are available on credit terms. Advertising is also playing a growing role in the consumer economy.

As the economy has developed, so have the sources of prestige. Conspicuous consumption is a major new source of prestige, but it is only one of several. Conspicuous public service is another. People like the doctor and Humberto Soto (discussed more fully in chapter 10) are highly esteemed for their leadership. Humberto is often pointed out as an important local figure, even though supporting 10 children on a teacher's salary leaves him a skimpy surplus for consumption. Conspicuous *investment* is another source of public esteem, one that often precedes conspicuous consumption. Diplomas, for example, are prized possessions to be proudly displayed on living-room walls. Some families have a half-dozen or more: children's primary certificates, secondary diplomas, correspondence school diplomas, certificates of competence in shorthand or typing—any symbol that the family has made a successful commitment to modern life.

The inauguration of the Calzado Nacional on the main street in 1970 is a more dramatic example of investment and prestige in San Pedro society. The Calzado Nacional is a very special building—the first three-story building erected in the department of San Marcos. It is also a symbol to San Pedranos, who are fond of boasting that their town, and not the department capital or one of the large coastal towns, was the first to have such structure. The building was inaugurated with grand ceremony; its owner hired a marimba orchestra, prepared a feast, and invited important people. The local radio station broadcast the music, as well as the speeches of local dignitaries all applauding the young owner's magnificient labor. One speaker was particularly emphatic.

"This building," he said for all the community to hear, "should stand as an example to all San Pedranos of the right and proper way to use their money."

And why should the conspicuous ownership of capital not have a prestige component, just like the conspicuous ownership of luxury goods? A truck is a powerful, visible, modern item that brings its owner wealth and security. For San Pedranos, in fact, trucks are an important index of wealth. One campesino interrogated me on the conditions of life in the United States—even rustic Guatemalans are fascinated with the place—asking if it were not true that the United States was so prosperous that "everyone owns at least one truck." Truck owners, likewise, readily admit their pride in owning and understanding such marvelous equipment. What is true of trucks is also true of stores, diplomas, and other kinds of new capital, as well as new durable goods. "What people want around here," a townswoman summarized, "is an education, a good business, or a fine house."

The growing economy has further amplified sources of prestige by diversifying labor. In San Miguel, every man is a farmer, and no man is sufficiently wealthy to control permanently the labor of others. When a Miguelense campesino hires a neighbor to help with cultivation, he does so on a temporary basis, and he himself participates in the work. A patrón in contrast, rarely weaves himself—as the capitalist his role is permanently different and his status permanently higher. He is truly a patrón and is so addressed by his workers. Truckers are also addressed as "patrón" by their drivers and loaders.

Luxury consumption is also growing spectacularly. A "fine house" by current San Pedro standards is made of brick, with tile floors, plumbing, and window glass. A few people own luxury cars. Stylish modern clothing is becoming fashionable for both men and women. I seldom saw people dressed in rags; most San Pedranos have a graded wardrobe containing work clothes, casual wear, and festive clothes. Domestic expenditures for household applicances and furnishings are increasing.

From observation of individual cases, it seems to be that consumption desires developed in San Pedro after entrepreneurial investment was well under way. As an entrepreneur the Indian is capable of foregoing consumption while he builds his business—a telling factor in ethnic competition, as we shall see. Anselmo exemplifies this. Although his holdings are extensive, he lives much like an Indian, eating and dressing simply and passing his days oblivious to the necessity of, say, a new dining-room set. His innocent happiness, however, is about to end. Brother German lives more elegantly, being broadly traveled and married to a Ladina, and Anselmo's Indian wife is intrigued by the finery of his household. In other families it is the youngsters with civilizado and Ladino school chums to impress who exert the pressure to spend *papacito's* new wealth on luxury goods. By such complicated routes the consumer spirit enters traditional society.

Economic Development and Indian Personality

The same new opportunities that have increased his wealth have also changed the San Pedrano's personality, which is now remarkably different from that of Indians in more isolated communities. Latin American Indians are characteristically shy and unassertive in public situations or when interacting with social superiors. They manifest a kind of split personality: in the security of their communities the true personality of each man emerges, and these personalities are as diverse as in any human group, but in dealing with outsiders even the boldest Indian tends to be withdrawn and timid. All interpersonal diversity becomes submerged in a cowed and servile public self. This widespread social character, which Erasmus has labeled the *encogido* syndrome (1968), predominates in San Miguel. Miguelenses who are proud of their bravery, for example, boast that they are not afraid to "enter any office," this being their measure of courage. Some San Pedranos, especially aldean campesinos, still display traces of this Indian reserve, but many appear totally free of it.

I once attended a dinner held by several dozen San Pedranos of all occupations. The town doctors were there, business people, and a number of artisans. Conviviality and camaraderie reigned. The guests talked, joked, and drank at length, and several men, with great feeling and drama, read selections of original poetry. Even though the entire proceedings were being taped for rebroadcast on local radio, there was no hint of hesitation or insecurity in any of the participants' behavior. On other occasions, I have seen townsmen of all occupations address large audiences with similar aplomb.

There is also a startling contrast between the personalities of San Pedro women and interior Indian women, who are even more painfully withdrawn than the men. San Pedro has already produced a myriad of women schoolteachers and some notable female entrepreneurs. It is an interesting Latin American paradox that, despite the restricted traditional position of women, they are not barred from playing an important role in developing economies. Once again, the personality transformation of San Pedro women is far from complete—especially in the aldeas—but San Pedranas tend to manifest an openness and often an aggressive flirtatiousness virtually unknown among their rural sisters.

This change more than any of the others, going to the core of the Indians' identity, reveals the pervasive effects of San Pedro's economic development. The mental and social closure of the peasant community diminishes in a developing economy. Commercialization in San Pedro has forced people into new social roles. Truckers, store owners, and patrons, in their travels around the country, must constantly deal with strangers, which reinforces their self-confidence. Education likewise promotes geographical mobility and contact with an extended range of people, with the bonus of broadening awareness through study. Development thus creates new social roles and encourages new kinds of experiences, with profound effect on self-image.

The interplay of personality and experience emerges dramatically from the biography of a San Pedrano who has experienced a meteoric change in status. Marcos Fuentes was born in San Pedro in 1916, the son of a farmer. Through good fortune and determination he was able to educate himself and now holds a high post in the Ministry of Agriculture in Guatemala City. Marcos has always been acutely aware of his Indianness, and even today as a grown man in a prestigious position he occasionally manifests encogido behavior. He still recalls with painful vividness the shock of leaving his Indian home at 12 years of age to study agronomy in Quezaltenango. Being one of two Indians in a school of over 100 students was traumatic. His Indian companion had it worse than he did, being more obviously Indian in appearance, speech, and name, but both were subjected to cruel bullying and racial taunts.

Marcos remembers having two particular problems during his school years, the first being what he calls a *complejo de inferioridad*. A sense of inferiority is part of being Indian, he believes, and his was compounded by the trauma of entering a new, competitive, and hostile social situation. He still recalls how his talent in mathematics helped assuage this complex by giving him objective proof of his capabilities and allowing him to win friends by aiding his *compañeros* with their homework. He suffered also from diffuse and pervasive insecurity, especially during his first years in school. The cultural gap between the group he had left and the one he was entering was great, provoking a period of shock while he learned how to wear a suit and tie, where to sit in a theater, the ins and outs of Ladino etiquette.

Today, he says, with schooling, reading, and international travel behind him, he is generally comfortable and secure even around high-powered professional associates. Only when conversation diverges from agronomy onto less familiar ground does he feel twinges of inadequacy.

No one tells the story of Marco's success better than he. It begins in 1928,

> when I was studying sixth grade in the national boys school of San Pedro Sacatepéquez. The sixth-grade teacher was accustomed to stimulate and test the capacity of the students by means of verbal competitions. The process consisted of fighting for first place by answering questions.
>
> Of all the students in the class, the brothers Vidal and Augustín Fuentes were consistently the best, always winning the first and second prizes. Unfortunately, these two talented brothers were, for economic reasons, forced to retire from school at the beginning of June of that year. Some ten days after their departure from school, the government of the Republic offered a scholarship for the best student to continue his studies in the National Agricultural School in Quezaltenango. As the brothers were no longer enrolled, I was favored with the scholarship. The Fuentes brothers, meanwhile, began working in manual labor to help their parents with the needed household income.

Marcos's studies carried him far. After receiving a degree in agronomy in 1934 he worked for a time on coffee plantations and then as professor in the Escuela Central de Agricultura. In 1944 he received another scholarship, this time from the U.S. Department of Agriculture, and spent a year in the United States specializing in soil conservation.

> On my return I took up teaching again, until June 1946, when I was appointed director of the Department of Soil Conservation of the Ministry of Agriculture.
>
> As director, my travels took me back to San Pedro where I had the opportunity to again meet my friends the Fuentes brothers, who were still in manual occupations and earning the pitiful salaries of 30 cents a day. Since it was within my possibilities to help them, I offered them work in our projects, with salaries that shortly rose to two quetzals a day, because of their quick intelligence.
>
> When we first encountered each other, I was shocked by the extreme humility of these old friends, who now insisted on addressing me as *don*. I suggested that such behavior was inappropriate, and that they treat me with the friendship and familiarity of previous times.

The lives of these three men of similar background and intelligence diverged radically because of a chance event in 1928. Had the Fuentes brothers stayed in school but another few weeks, one of them, rather than Marcos, would have benefited from free higher education and become the confident, self-assured individual. Confined by their menial occupations, the unfortunate Fuentes brothers retained the humility of their forebears.

Change in San Pedro's Aldeas

The valley and ridges surrounding the twin cities are dotted with small hamlets that belong, culturally and administratively, to either the municipio of San Marcos or the municipio of San Pedro. In this section I describe the continuum of change that now characterizes hamlets of San Pedro Sacatepéquez. San Pedro administers 17 hamlets, each of which has its own auxiliary government and school. In none has civilización proceeded as far as it has in the cabecera, but some are notably more progressive than others. The aldeas arrange themselves in a kind of folk-urban continuum, the more progressive ones clustering close to the town and the conservative ones lying in the remote hinterland. Distance is the major feature affecting access to town. The people of San José Caben can stroll to market or school in less than half an hour, while the journey from Sacachum Dolores takes almost four hours.

People of the aldeas, in general, display many outward signs of Indian conservatism. Women adhere to traditional dress more strongly than in the cabecera. People are more withdrawn and timid; it takes much longer to get to know them—especially in the remote aldeas. Horticulture is their primary occupation, augmented in some aldeas with handicrafts and mule trade. Aldean people also have a stronger sense of being naturales.

But aldean people are beginning to modernize in various ways. In all hamlets people now speak Spanish, and they are beginning to spend more of their income on housing and small luxuries. Even in faraway Petz, growing numbers of people are purchasing radios, and three families have recently floored their houses in concrete.

Despite their overall similarities, the aldeas are in many ways distinct. Each has adopted a slightly different selection of modern lifeways, so each seems to have developed a peculiar cultural set, almost a community personality, that local people can readily outline. Champollop, for example, has many Protestants, San José Caben a few, and Chamac almost none—though these hamlets are equally close to the cabecera. Chamac and San José Caben are the "rich" aldeas, Chamac being the richer, and both are centers of weaving.

Textile production in the other aldeas is weak or nonexistent. Three aldean men own trucks, all of them Chamaquenses. The people of San José are most "awake" to the value of education, sending dozens of students to San Marcos and San Pedro schools. La Grandeza and San Andrés Chápil, similarly close to the center, are still "asleep."

Each aldea constitutes a community in that it has a name, boundary, administrative organization, and independent fiesta system. There is, nevertheless, considerable social interaction between aldeas; they are not as socially circumscribed as the traditional municipio (Tax 1937, 1941). People regularly choose mates and *compadres* from other aldeas, sometimes own land in other aldeas, and kin (even close kin) often reside in different communities. There is consequently much visiting between aldeas. On occasion, men request to serve the image of a neighboring communty if they are particularly devoted to that image.

The social organization that interconnects the aldean populations extends to the cabecera as well. The town is not socially broken off from its hinterland; there are close connections of kinship and friendship between the two zones and considerable movement back and forth. Aldean people see the town not as an oppressive center of authority and discrimination, but as an exciting place to go on Sunday afternoons or during fiestas. Many also consider the town a desirable place to live, a view that has prompted significant urban migration. Aldean men often serve in municipal civic posts, and previously served occasionally as cofrades of town images. People in San José Caben once served Corpus Cristi of the central church for seven years running.

Town and countryside are also connected through participation in formal organizations. Most of the membership of town religious, civic, and scholastic institutions is drawn from the town itself, but a significant amount now comes from aldean populations, as the growth of Protestantism and educational interest in certain communities indicates. Two lay Catholic organizations, Acción Católica and the Tercera Orden Franciscana, have strong aldean representation, as do the hermandades. Again, the degree of participation in these organizations varies considerably between aldeas and tends to be strongest in those closer to town. In the remote aldeas, voluntary organizations and organizational participation are strictly local. Almost no one leaves the community to study, worship, or engage in politics.

Political awareness and activity display a similar pattern: San José Caben and Chamac have long histories of progressive public action; Petz lags well behind. The people of San José began forming improvement committees in the late 1940s and have successfully completed numerous projects. They have cobbled their streets, built a new school with five grades, and installed potable water and electricity. The people of Petz have none of these facilities (other than a three-grade school, which virtually every rural hamlet now has) but they are beginning to aspire to them. When I visited the hamlet, men were talking of forming a Comité pro Mejoramiento (betterment committee), and the aldean authority had already requested a government water survey.

Modernization, in summary, is spreading to the San Pedro hinterland. Its effects can be seen everywhere, though they are decidedly weaker in the aldeas remote from the stimulus of the town. The closer aldeas, San José Caben, Chamac, and to a lesser degree Champollop, have more complex, stronger economies, greater numbers of progressive individuals, and more effective political organizations. Of all the aldeas, these most resemble what San Pedro is today. The remote aldeas are less developed and more self-sufficient socially and economically, and are contemporary replicas of what San Pedro was before the era of social awakening.

Notes

[1]Bodegas are informal stores, storerooms actually, without display counters or cash registers. Their owners specialize in some product or series of products, and most of their business is wholesale.

[2]All weaving in San Pedro is done on foot looms identical in basic design to those used in Europe before the Industrial Revolution. Looms are constructed and repaired by local carpenters. The only recent improvements in weaving technology have been the substitution of metal combs in the battens of the looms for earlier wooden ones, and the use of more varied, commercial yarns. Both of these changes have improved the quality and variety of cloth produced, but neither has substantially increased per capita output.

Major export products are bolt cloth, stoles, and *mañaneras,* a kind of light woman's poncho. Huipiles and skirts for the traditional San Pedrana costume are also produced. Cloth is woven in every imaginable color, and decorated with a broad variety of natural and geometric designs. The possibility that this industry will be disrupted by mechanization is slight, according to local people. Master weavers tell me that the designs they produce are so complex that they could only be reproduced by the most complicated of machine looms.

TEN

Social Change in San Pedro

Economic growth has been the dominant influence in San Pedro in recent decades, just as population growth has been the dominant influence in San Miguel. The new wealth, knowledge, and roles that constitute this economic expansion have markedly altered community social organization. In this chapter I discuss changes in community organization, mobility patterns, and emulation, and changes in ethnic relations, particularly those between San Pedranos and the Ladinos of neighboring San Marcos.

Social Organization and Mobility

There are two principal social cleavages in the present-day municipal population, both of recent origin. One divides the population into two locally recognized cultural classes: the so-called civilized people and the naturales. These terms denote differing cultural orientations symbolized by style of dress and housing, refinement of speech and manners, and general level of cosmopolitanism. The other social cleavage results from differences in wealth. Although the town has always been stratified, wealth differences among Indians have become more extreme in recent years. The major difference between present and traditional stratification patterns is that although economic evolution has generally elevated the material welfare of the population, it has not done so equally. Virtually everyone has benefited from recent development, but some people, especially the mercantile capitalists, have benefited fabulously.

The term "civilizado" (or "gente civilizada") designates people who are indigenous by race but modern by culture. The term is used by local people themselves, in preference to labels such as *indígena* and especially *indio,* which they consider imprecise and insulting. Ladinos employ the label civilizado less frequently. A Quezaltenango Ladino who resides in San Pedro, for example, refers to the local people indiscriminately as indígenas, and I have even heard him call the super-rich Indians of Quezaltenango *inditos millonarios* (roughly, little Indian millionaires). An educated San Pedrano on the other hand, explains the process of civilización this way: "those who are civilized are those who have had some schooling, have changed their customs a little, and have entered the orbit of a moderately high culture. These people go along adopting new systems and are able to relate to Ladino people." Marcos Fuentes is an ideal example of a *natural* who has become highly civilizado.

Economic and cultural groups overlap significantly, since there are many naturales who are considerably wealthier than most civilized people. The wealthiest people, in fact—the truckers, textile merchants, and large store owners—tend to be rugged, rustic individuals, many of whom, like Anselmo, are minimally educated. "Civilización" requires around six years of education, but this amount of schooling does not always lead to great wealth. Of the civilized people who have not emigrated from the community, only the doctor and a handful of lawyers have incomes that even approach those of prosperous merchants.

Growing income, however, invariably brings civilización in the second generation. Gumercindo Miranda owns three almacenes, two in San Pedro and one in the coastal town of Malacatán. His principal store, previously the property of an Italian, is one of the largest in San Pedro. Although a highly successful businessman, Gumercindo is a *natural* by local classification. His educated daughter, who dresses in modern fashions and speaks literate Spanish, is *civilizada*. Her children will also be civilizados, and, people say, she is even improving the behavior of her parents.

The roots of the movement toward civilización are deep, since education was the first of the profitable new resources that San Pedranos uncovered. Modern educational aspirations began before the Depression. Several local people earned teaching degrees in the early years of this century. Two men earned law degrees in the early 1920s, and later served as municipal mayors. During the Ubico period, three men rose to the rank of colonel in the Guatemalan military, having gotten their start with state scholarships to the national military academy. During the 1930s and especially the 1940s, educational aspirations grew, bolstered by the opening of the public normal school in San Marcos around 1945.

With the multiplication of educational facilities over the last decade, San Pedranos no longer need to be wealthy to educate their children, so the *civilizado-natural* boundary will gradually dissolve in the coming years. The desire for education is already spreading in the adjacent aldeas, initiating the slow process of cultural transformation that is aleady so advanced in town. In the near future, probably only Sacuchúm Dolores, Santa Teresa, and other remote aldeas will remain as pockets of *natural* culture. The families of these peripheral communities are so remote from the spirit and facilities of the town that their attitudes on education resemble those of Miguelenses more than those of urban San Pedranos.

This educational boundary, in which Petz and other remote aldeas are on the San Miguel rather than the San Pedro side of the fence, is an interesting case of multicausal social patterning. Scholastic ambition and participation are strongest among residents (both Ladino and Indian) of the San Marcos-San Pedro urban center, and are growing in aldeas that are within walking distance of central schools. Beyond this zone, it becomes more expensive to educate children because of transportation and boarding costs. Feasible commuting distance for pedestrians seems to be about four kilometers at maximum, on level terrain. Even rural Ladinos living beyond this boundary are undereducated.

There is also a motivational threshold, congruent with the geographical boundary. By and large, people living outside commuting distance are not interested in educating their children; they see no value or reward in it. Education is of much greater benefit to the one who studies than to the one who pays. The rural peasant would earn no material rewards for shouldering the burden of a son's education, nor would he be congratulated by his community, which places its values elsewhere. Furthermore, the expense would be undertaken at great risk, since the peasant has few means to judge his child's scholastic potential, and no hard evidence that a man in his position, from his village, can successfully finance such an undertaking. Besides, education, as a thing of economic worth, is but vaguely comprehended by rural people. How many years of study are necessary? What payoff can be expected from various amounts of schooling? How much will costs increase as the student advances? Evaluating such questions is difficult for isolated rural people.

I studied the histories of 26 professional people who are considered to be outstanding progressives. All but one are townsmen. Nine of these people presently live in San Pedro, and 16 elsewhere (one is deceased). Eleven are teachers, five are lawyers, three are colonels, and two are doctors. One is an engineer and one an accountant. The oldest received his degree in 1921, and several of the younger individuals are now working as teachers while studying law in the evenings.

The divergent family backgrounds of these people demonstrate the general availability of educational opportunity in San Pedro. The 26 individuals come from 16 families, of which five were civilizado and 11 *natural* in the preceding generation. Only three of the *natural* families were wealthy; the others were families of craftsmen and campesinos, most of whom were illiterate. Only six of the 26 students were supported by the state during their schooling. Ten received help from their families, many of whom deprived themselves in order to aid their sons, and 10 financed their education through personal effort. All of these people are renowned and highly esteemed by the community: those who won scholarships are esteemed for their aptitude, those supported by their families for familial dedication to modernization, and those who rose on their own for their drive and ambition.

The emergence of educated people and the decision by many of them to reside in their native town has created a culturally plural society in what was previously an Indian municipio. But it is a unique plural society in that both cultural communities within it share a sense of Indian identity and local social attachment. The town doctor, for example, despite his education and wealth, never attempts to hide his Indian heritage. He frankly admits that he is the son of Mam-speaking campesinos and comerciantes. On one occasion, he publicly defended his community against the racial taunts of certain Ladinos, explaining over local radio that there are no differences between Indians and Ladinos from a medical point of view, and that what bothered San Pedranos most about their race was that their Indian blood was not as pure as they would like it to be. He even displays a family "coat of arms" in his living room, consisting of a large wooden shield emblazoned with a book and the head of a hoe. These things, he says, epitomize his history.

The community involvement and the spirit of prominent persons such as the doctor—the very fact that he prefers to live and work among his native people, rather than in the capital—creates a social climate that encourages mobility. The pluralism of San Pedro is not stagnant and exploitative; it is one of the bases of continuing community advance. Naturales are encouraged to participate in progressive activities by three significant conditions: the openness of voluntary organizations, the civic participation of educated individuals, and the character of interpersonal relations between the gente civilizada and the gente natural.

San Pedro is a highly organized town, especially for a rural community in a preindustrial nation. The community is laced together by a surprising complex of civic organizations, religious sodalites, youth clubs, and neighborhood improvement committees. Much of this organization has been inspired and promoted by the gente civilizada. As early as the 1920s, several educated people collaborated to organize a workers' association to improve the conditions and education of people in manual occupations. This association, the Sociedad de Obreros, still exists. The Casa de la Cultura Sampedrana is an even more impressive example of organizational openness. When town leaders were approached about founding a local chapter of the international Club de Leones (Lions Club), they felt that the national club directorship was pressuring them to set up an elitist organization that would exclude participation by naturales or nonprofessionals. Rejecting the club, they founded the Casa de la Cultura, which is now an autonomous civic organization working for cultural and economic progress in the whole community. Its directorship during my stay was drawn from various occupations: two doctors, one lawyer, five merchants, and five craftsmen. The new religious brotherhoods are likewise nondiscriminatory and provide an important social link between townsmen and residents of nearby hamlets, since a significant number of members are drawn from these communities. Both the leadership and membership of the brotherhoods also come from many occupational groups.

As they did with the Casa de la Cultura and the Sociedad de Obreros, educated people regularly provide civic leadership. In most cases they have done so without pay, out of a sense of public duty. Humberto Soto was one of the first people from cantón La Independencia to complete his secondary education. After teaching for 12 years in an interior municipio, he obtained a post in San Pedro and returned to his cantón. Soon he began teaching basic literacy in his neighborhood, free of charge and on his own time. "They were my neighbors," he explains, "and they did not know how to read." Though some of his students wanted to reward him with gifts, he convinced them that their enthusiasm could better be channeled into public works. Three hundred men responded to his call to repair the much-traveled but muddy main street of the cantón, and Humberto subsequently organized a permanent neighborhood-betterment committee. In working with his neighborhood and with the Casa de la Cultura, Humberto has found local people both eager for improvements and capable of financing them. Their only need is sophisticated leadership.

Relationships between gente civilizada and naturales are generally cordial and respectful. Although the former maintain a certain social distance from the latter, they do so without the displays of superiority and contempt that characterize Ladino treatment of Indians. The interaction of a civilized town family and a campesino family from a nearby hamlet, both of whom I was able to observe closely, is a case in point. The town family considers itself a member of the town *sociedad,* and prefers to exclude even familiar naturales from family celebrations. Naturales are never present at these events except as servants. The aldean family, on the other hand, regularly invites members of the town family to its festivities, and the town family always complies. Members of the aldean family drop by the town house daily, to chat or leave bundles, and are always treated cordially. All members of both families address all adults of both families as *don* and *doña,* even though the country people are naturales and the country wife still wears traditional costume. The town family did not consider the country family to be stepping out of place in enrolling one of its sons in the San Marcos military academy; on the contrary, they are proud of this display of progressive initiative.

The community elite is consequently more a target for emulation than a social barrier. Even illiterate men such as Virgilio, a brickmaker from Chamac, can aspire to personal betterment. Virgilio is much impressed by German Orozco, whose success he attributes to education and worldy experience. Virgilio himself was an orphan with no schooling. When he had the chance to study in the army, he felt so "useless" and ashamed of his ignorance that he could not bring himself to attend class. But he still has plans and aspirations for his children, because he knows that "German's father was a simple man, just like me." His sons consider brickmaking shameful, dirty, and grueling, so with Virgilio's aid they are learning to weave as a way to finance secondary educations. This tactic of working half-time at some craft and studying in the afternoons or evenings is common among young San Pedranos. The opportunities are there for anyone with the desire to change, and the example presented by successful people is gradually intensifying this desire.

Relations with San Marcos

Relations between the Indian population of San Pedro and the Ladino population of San Marcos have always been tense, and occasionally violent—one person, at least, has lost his life in the ongoing feud between the two towns.

Even in the last century this tension was serious enough to attract national attention. In 1876, President Barrios passed a law declaring the Indians of San Pedro officially Ladino and permitting them to wear Ladino dress. Apparently, local people say, the government thought it could solve the ethnic problem by officially merging the ethnic groups.[1] Unfortunately, this tactic was ineffective. San Pedranos to this day feel that they have been continuously and systematically exploited, dominated, and mistreated by Marquenses. In the past, they were unable to respond except through sporadic violence, but in recent years they have developed a new sense of power and are replacing their old feelings of subjugation with new competitive ones. "We have always been mistreated by the Ladino," a community leader said, "but we have never liked it. Now, with the social awakening, we will dominate them—but we will do it culturally." By that he means that they intend to supersede San Marcos as the principal town of the region.

The new Indian sense of power stems in part from their manifest accomplishments, many of them more impressive than those of San Marcos. So secure have San Pedranos become in their progress that they occasionally hold their neighbors up to ridicule and contempt. Marquenses, they say, are all *políticos* working in salaried jobs, maneuvering for bribes and sinecures, while San Pedranos are self-made and independent. San Marcos is dull and dead, but San Pedro is *alegre,* bustling. It is a common San Pedro joke that at 8:00 p.m. one can walk naked through the streets of San Marcos without being seen.

As Indian ambitions have grown, ethnic competition has intensified, espcially in schools and in business. In both areas the Indians are holding their own. Noon athletics in the normal school always pits San Pedranos against Marquenses, occasionally producing fist fights, and Indian students are still subject to racial jibes. But students say that such hostility no longer intimidates them "because we go to San Marcos *en fuerzu* (in force)." Marcos Fuentes, with his solitary Indian companion, would have benefited from the numerical strength that San Pedro students now enjoy.

Indians, in general, are also winning in their economic competition with Ladinos. With the exception of buses, the regional transport industry is now almost exclusively in Indian hands. Two Indian retailers have established outlets in San Marcos, but no Marquense has done so in San Pedro. Even immigrant merchants have trouble competing with Indians. Jorge Basila, a Lebanese, immigrated to San Marcos in 1933, where he opened a store selling imported cloth. As San Pedranos captured that business he was forced to change inventories, now handling furniture and automobile parts. *"No se puede competir con el indio,"* he says (one cannot compete with Indians).

As a result of San Pedro's economic growth, Ladinos also have difficulty competing with the Indians in the political sphere. Compared to smaller communities such as San Miguel, San Pedro enjoys three advantages that make it a formidable political adversary. These advantages are larger municipal revenues, better leadership, and more effective public involvement in municipal affairs. As economies develop and private incomes grow, so do tax bases. The economy of San Miguel is so attenuated that it provides little surplus for public use; the municipality must depend for revenue on a head tax and the scant funds it can wrest from federal agencies. In addition to the head tax, San Pedro taxes local businesses and industries according to their size, all trucks and taxis that park in town, and all buses that pass through (some 50 every day). Each vendor in both the mercado and the plaza pays a weekly tax, again according to the size of his operation, and each citizen pays subscription rates for household water and electricity. Such a large flow of revenue also makes the municipio an attractive, secure candidate for national development loans.

These revenues have been used to make significant improvements. The town has had electric power since 1910, and potable water since 1928 (San Miguel still has neither). During my stay the community completed a new primary school and a new bus terminal, and renovated the central park. An improved electrical network—power from dams on the coast to replace an obsolete local system—was being installed by the Instituto Nacional de Electrificación, and community leaders were discussing replacing the old mercado with a multistoried *centro comercial*. Shortly after I left, the major streets, previously cobbled, were resurfaced with asphalt. Even the aldeas of San Pedro are ahead of the municipio of San Miguel in establishing schools and public utilities.

Leadership in San Pedro long ago began the transformation from introspective traditionalism to worldly progress. Wealth and, more important, education have superseded age as the prerequisities of formal authority. Consuegra (n.d.:27) describes an earlier gerontocracy that was suppressed by the departmental governor in 1910:

> The *Principales* or *Cabezas Amarradas* (so called because of special turbans they wore) were the famous organization of genuine patriots of San Pedro Sacatepéquez. This organization of wise aboriginal character was composed of the most responsible citizens of the entire district, especially the oldest . . . The *Principales* or *Cabezas Amarradas* were

the citizens who disposed all of the works of the *pueblo,* the most urgent commissions to higher authorities, the defenses against epidemics, the defense of the jurisdictional boundaries with respect to neighboring *pueblos;* in short, the defense of the township in any circumstance (my translation).

From the turn of the century onward, the community benefited from the political leadership of its increasingly sophisticated elite. Many school-teachers, a few lawyers, and even one colonel have served as *alcalde munici-pal.* The immigrant merchants regularly held municipal office. As discussed earlier, the educated elite also made significant contributions, even when they were not holding formal office, by founding various civic betterment organizations. The participation of these men in public life has been a community resource of immeasurable value.

The activities of these leaders have been aided on the one hand by the substantial fiscal base of the community, and, on the other, by the people's general political awareness and propensity to organize. Although San Pedranos vary tremendously in their understanding and enthusiasm for national politics, the central location of the community and the greater impact of the media and of educated leadership have left them much more sophisticated than interior populations.

They are, besides, highly susceptible to organization and concerted community action. They even boast that they are much more civically active than the Marquenses, which seems to be true. Some years ago San Marcos received a grant of almost Q100,000 in the will of a descendant of Justo Rufino Barrios. A committee of prominent citizens "spent" a suspiciously large amount of the grant on a sports stadium, provoking outraged Marquenses to circulate a petition demanding open hearing on the use of the funds. But few of their fellow citizens would sign the petition, so the effort failed. The episode gained great local notoriety, and both San Pedranos and Marquenses believe that the failure of the Marquense pueblo to demand investigation was a result of that town's particular economic organization. When public service is the principal source of employment and advancement is based on a complex system of patronage and favoritism, it is foolish to embarass the powers that be. In San Pedro, business, not politics, is the most profitable field of activity, giving the individual greater freedom to engage in public affairs and to criticize public officials.

San Pedro's political power has also been boosted by emigration to Guatemala City. Literacy and modernization of the occupational structure have promoted considerable geographical mobility among San Pedranos, much of it to the capital. San Pedranos living in Guatemala City have formed the *Fraternidad Sampedrana* as a political lobby for their old community. When San Pedro was pushing to be included in the new electrical network, Fraternidad members followed up the formal petitions with phone calls and visits to the appropriate ministers. In a country with poor communications and a centralized government, such a lobby is a priceless resource.

San Pedro has now turned its political strength outward in its rivalry with San Marcos, as I learned on April 1, of 1970, when large crowds of Ladinos and Indians met in violent confrontation. Between the two towns lies a much-contested no man's land, a small zone containing the departmental capitol, the public health clinic, and a few residences and small businesses. A major boulevard traverses this zone, connecting the park of San Marcos with the plaza of San Pedro. Both municipios claim the zone and have been vying for its control since the 1940s. On this occasion, the San Pedranos were attempting to substantiate their claim by erecting street lights along the boulevard at their own public expense. They were vigorously opposed by the mayor of San Marcos, some of the citizens of San Marcos, and the departmental governor. The mayor of San Pedro advised them all that construction would continue and that if they interfered he would call out his pueblo to force the issue, which he finally did. What occurred subsequently was a unique display of Indian political determination.

The contested zone originated in Ladino attempts to merge the two communities into a single municipio. Reyna Barrios, president of Guatemala and native of San Marcos, made the first effort to unify the two municipios in 1893. In 1935 Ydígoras Fuentes, then *Jefe Político* of San Marcos under Ubico, proclaimed another edict declaring the "public utility and necessity" of implementing Reyna Barrios's resolution by forming Ciudad la Unión, with municipal and departmental offices on the site now in dispute. This site was expropriated from San Pedro territory, and over the next six years localities in the department were taxed a total of $13,780 for public buildings. From 1941 to 1945 San Pedro Sacatepéquez and San Marcos were legally conjoined and became known as the municipio San Marcos la Unión.

This unification met instant opposition from San Pedranos. However noble the idea, they felt it was detrimental to lose their autonomy. Their feelings were well grounded. They were never compensated for the expropriated land, and they lost control over their large tax revenues. Also the municipal reorganization was not the expressed will of either community; it

Figure 1. The old convent in Ixtahuacán, now under the firm control of the priest and the orthodox Catholic community.

Figure 2. Many young people in Ixtahuacán now speak Spanish and dress as Ladinos. These girls have just returned from Guatemala City, where they were working as maids.

Figure 3. Rural people in San Miguel identify themselves as Indians, dressing in Indian fashion and speaking Mam by preference.

Figure 4. The hamlet El Triunfo, marketplace for San Miguel. Every Saturday its plaza fills with truckers and peddlers from San Pedro, Tejutla, and other neighboring municipios.

Figure 5. An eroded hillside in San Miguel, previously a planted field. Note the deforestation of hillsides in the background.

Figure 6. A new house in San Miguel. One of the more substantial houses in hamlet Subchal, it has walls of whitewashed adobe and a floor of packed earth.

Figure 7. Many San Pedranos are craftsmen, such as carpenters.

Figure 8. This is a family of soapmakers. Rarely do San Pedro families support themselves from agriculture alone.

Figure 9. Textile arts such as weaving and knitting play a major role in San Pedro's economy.

Figure 10. These men have a successful tailoring shop.

Figure 11. San Pedro is a commercial center. Virtually all trade, from trucking to shopkeeping to peddling, is in Indian hands.

Figure 12. A shopkeeper in San Pedro.

Figure 13. The first three-story building in the Department of San Marcos was built by an Indian entrepreneur in San Pedro.

Figure 14. A new house in San Pedro. It is made of brick, with floors of ceramic tile.

did not originate in local referendum but in arbitrary decrees of Ladino authorities—which are automatically suspect among Indians. Talk of unified progress was camouflage, San Pedranos feared. In reality, unification would promote the development of San Marcos at the expense of San Pedro.

Agitation against the union reached an effective level shortly after the Revolution of 1944. Attempts to suppress San Pedro opposition had been met on one occasion with violence, when the police were stoned by an angry Indian crowd. An underground party, the Partido Arevalista, was working against the union, and the revolutionary government received regular requests for separation, among them a petition of over 1000 signature. Marquenses, too, began to favor separtion when rumors spread that the Indians were on the verge of riot. Fear of bloodshed provoked the Arévalo government to dissolve the union in the famous degree of 1944.

But rather than resolving the problem, this clumsy, self-contradictory decree extend it. One clause clearly stated that all borders were to be returned to their pre-Unión positions (thus returning to San Pedro its territory), while another gave San Marcos jurisdiction over public works in the intervening zone. San Pedrano leaders see this as a clear violation of the national constitution: one township cannot be given authority in the territory of another.

Hence the San Pedrano street-light gambit and hence the Marquense resistance. Two lampposts had been erected, and the third was going in under the very windows of the governor's office when the brief battle was joined. A large crowd of Indians faced a much smaller one of Ladinos. Policemen and soldiers milled around ineffectively. The two groups exchanged taunts and Marquense tempers rose at the outrageous incursion into "their" territory. In a hasty conference, the governor agreed that the third post could be raised if the mayor of San Pedro would agree to a 24-hour "truce" in which the problem could be discussed. San Pedranos were delighted and hoisted the mayor to their shoulders. Marquenses, enraged, showered the Indians with rocks and fled under the return volley. One San Pedrano was hospitalized with a headwound.

That evening a town meeting was called, and the municipal auditorium filled to capacity. Leaders outlined the issues and their decision to continue the fight. Several years ago, the mayor said, San Marcos had introduced its water system into the zone, with the support of the governor. San Pedrano objections were met with appeals to reason. According to one Indian leader:

When they want to do something, they call on us to be civilized and brotherly and to favor progress. When we want to do something similar, they call us indios and accuse us of *localismo* and of being uncultured.

The doctor said the issue should have been resolved long ago, but the authorities were afraid ''to touch the ember.'' Now, he said, it was a Supreme Court case, and legal aid could be had ''at any moment.'' A court battle was within the social and economic reach of the community.

The microphone was opened to the audience and many individuals spoke, some denouncing the Marquenses, some ridiculing them, but all in favor of continuing the fight. ''We are no longer indios and they are not going to deceive us again.'' ''We are through,'' said another, ''with mistreatment from those *españoles* with their white faces.'' The president of the Sociedad de Obreros declared his organization's support of the mayor's action. The next day the municipality declared the departmental governor *persona non grata* in San Pedro, and he was soon removed from office. There the matter stood when I left the field.

The San Pedranos' dedication to winning is out of proportion to the economic value of the territory in dispute. The land has become a symbol for them, and the feud is fired by all the injustices, real and assumed, that they have ever suffered at the hands of Marquenses. But their contentiousness is instructive in that it is so sustained, versatile, and organized. Traditional Indians are capable of sporadic resistance; they explode, gain nothing, and live with their frustration. San Pedranos have fought this battle for three decades, and can envision carrying it to the Supreme Court. Win or lose, they have shown their ability to fight with the Ladinos' own weapons.

Notes

[1]The decree reads in part that the *''indígenas* of both sexes of the aforementioned *pueblo* of San Pedro Sacatepéquez are declared Ladinos, and shall use from the coming year onward the dress corresponding to the Ladino class'' (Consuegra n.d.:22). Jorge Ubico rescinded this decree in the 1930s, ''because they continue being *indígena,* with native costume.''

ELEVEN

Fiesta Reorganization
in San Miguel Ixtahuacán

The food and money that Indians consume to honor their saints consists of "surplus" productivity. It is income over and above the minimum needed to sustain the lives of the people who produce it (Wolf 1966:5-6). As subsistence economies degenerate, ceremonial surpluses become harder and harder to raise, a situation that threatens the fiesta system by intensifying the inherent costs of ritual giving. This chapter discusses how the fiesta system changes under conditions of economic crisis.

Costs and Incentives in San Miguel Ixtahuacán

In the recent history of San Miguel, fewer and fewer people have had agricultural surpluses to commit to public display. Agriculture has been supplemented to an ever-greater extent by wage labor, and farming is no longer a source of surplus wealth. For most families, excess income to meet communal obligations can be accumulated only by expanding the debilitating, hated occupation of wage work.

The scarcity of surpluses and the difficulty of raising them have intensified and broadened resistance to cofradía service in San Miguel. They have rendered nonparticipation more desirable. The ideological and social differentiation of the community, along with alterations in local power, have made nonparticipation easier. Between them, these factors have shifted the contingencies of allocative choice away from those that characterized the traditional peasant community and also those that characterized San Miguel earlier in its history.

From the latter half of the 1930s to the present, the people of the various

villages of San Miguel have been simplifying their ceremonial organizations
to bring them more in line with their present capabilities. Structural simplification began after the intendente Adelberto Reyes distributed the images
among the aldeas. The effect of his action was to decentralize the organization, replacing the traditional municipio-wide organization with numerous
smaller ones. When each aldea was given responsibility for the festivity of a
particular image, it was also given the opportunity to celebrate it as grandly or
as parsimoniously as it pleased and to finance the celebration as it saw fit.

One would think that this immediate transfer of authority from the
municipal to the aldean level would give rise to greater diversity in ceremonial
forms, as each aldea developed its own variation. Actually, the trend of
change in all aldeas has been remarkably uniform. In all cases: (1) the number
of festive events celebrated each year has been reduced, (2) the complexity of
individual events has been reduced, and (3) several plans have been adopted
to distribute the costs of ceremonial observances among larger numbers of
people. All these serve to reduce the individual burden of ritual sponsorship.

The first step was taken by aldea La Patria, shortly after it was allocated
the image of Jesús Nazareno. A few years after receiving the image, the aldea
petitioned the intendente to return it to the cabecera, saying no one in the
hamlet was interested in its celebration. The image has been lodged in a side
altar of the church in Ixtahuacán ever since.

All other aldeas supported their new images, but in modified form. An
early change adopted in all communities was to continue choosing two men to
be responsible for each festivity, but to lighten their load by having every
family in the aldea contribute 25 cents and a few pounds of corn to a
ceremonial fund. This system of financing broke down rapidly in all but three
hamlets. Most aldeas experienced difficulty in convincing all their inhabitants
to contribute. Some people would skirt their obligation one way or another,
antagonizing the faithful contributors. General ill will developed within the
communities as a result of the dissatisfaction with the contribution system,
and it was finally rejected almost everywhere. Only in the hamlets of Sícabe
El Colmito, and Xponá, does the public still contribute toward fiesta costs.

In El Colmito collection was effected in a unique way, which may have
contributed to the success of the system there. Aldean officials would collect
an annual corn tax from all residents, allocating a portion to the cofrades. The
cofrades themselves then only had to collect enough money to supplement the
Q20 to Q40 they themselves were expected to contribute. Residents of El
Colmito complain, however, that despite the aid of the authorities not every-

one can be made to contribute their share. In Sícabe and Xponá the long-term stability of the collection system may have been aided by the slightly greater productivity of the region in which they are located (Xponá adjoins Sícabe).

The inherent difficulties in this contribution system are easy to understand. In a face-to-face community, people can easily keep track of one another's participation. If cofrades are continually rebuffed or evaded by certain people, the entire community soon knows of it. Those who have done their part become righteously indignant and are potentially hostile to the entire institution. Commitment to the organization is weakened by the feeling that costs are unjustly distributed.

To overcome this difficulty, several aldeas chose to return to the old sponsored system, but with more sponsors for each event. That way, it was felt, individual burdens would be less than under the original two-sponsor arrangement, while families could not avoid thier obligations since all would be selected in turn. In aldeas Chílibe, Subchal, Cabajchúm, and El Zapote four cofrades were to be appointed each year. In the municipal cabecera, which had responsibility for the fiesta patronal, the number of sponsors was raised to eight since this celebration is so large and costly. These appended organizations appeared at different times over the last three decades. Aldea Subchal began nominating four sponsors per fiesta at least 16 years ago, while in El Triunfo the collection system was still operating in 1964, when thieves administered the *coup de grace* to conspicuous giving in that hamlet by stealing the community's image.

El Triunfo offers a good example of the bitterness and strife that can develop over contributions. Eugenio Bautista and a friend were designated cofrades in El Triunfo in the early 1960s, with the right to collect among the entire hamlet to help meet expenses. The community was celebrating two events per year at the time, one on the day of Corpus Cristi, the other during the fiesta patronal. Both events took place in a casa de cofradía in the cabecera. Before the fiesta of Corpus Christi, the cofrades managed to collect a total of Q12 from their neighbors. At 25 cents per contribution, this means that 48 families, about one-third of the village, gave monetary assistance to their delegates. Things were worse before the fiesta patronal because many of the villagers had left for the fincas and were not available to either finance or enjoy the fiesta. This round of collecting netted them only Q2. In order to meet the communal responsibility to image and tradition, Eugenio and friend were forced to spend Q50 of their own money.

The experience left Eugenio disgusted and alienated. He felt that he had been obligated by the group to perform a service that the group did not want or respect. Rather than courteous compliance, he met resistance in his attempts to elicit aid. The ritual acts seemed to be hollow, pointless posturings since so many people did not attend. How could he feel he was contributing to the sacred security of his neighbors when most of them were uninterested in his efforts? And where was his reward, the esteem and gratitude that should follow public sacrifice?

For Eugenio, sponsorship was not the bittersweet experience it was in traditional peasant communities, where the pain of heavy expenditure was overlain with social and spiritual gratification. It was all cost and no reward, a drama without applause. He was glad, he says, when the image was stolen and the fiestas terminated, even though it seems unthinkable that an Indian could be relieved at the loss of an icon. The costumbre died *por la gracia de Dios,* he told me. *Ahora la aldea de Triunfo está libre, está suelto sin cargo* (Now the hamlet of Triunfo is free, free without a burden).

His attitude is shared by many of the people of his hamlet, who, though they have made a few half-hearted attempts to solicit a free image from the wife of the president of the Republic, have not yet replaced their saint. Three other hamlets (Cabajchúm, El Zapote, and Chílibe) have also had their images stolen in recent years, and only Chílibe has purchased a replacement. The others simply let the whole institution expire. *Ya olvidaron ellos* (they have already forgotten), an old man from El Zapote said of his neighbors' interest in public ritual.

Truly conservative, traditional Indians would be shocked at the callous indifference of Miguelenses to the loss of sacred objects. It is interesting to compare the reaction in these villages with that of the people of Zinacantán, who also recently lost a religious relic. In July 1970 I visited Chiapas on my return from Guatemala, being particularly interested in visiting Zinacantán. Evon Vogt was in the field at the time, and he counseled me to be cautious, as the municipio was still agitated over the recent theft of a chalice from the central church. Since tennis-shoe prints were found around the church, some Indians suspected that anthropologists were the culprits. One of the Harvard Project's major informants told me that he had found himself in some danger in the community because of his involvement with the anthropologists. Three months after the robbery, municipal authorities were still recording license numbers of all cars that entered the community, and guards were patrolling at night with guns. In Zinacantán, religious robbery is not cause for relief but for outrage and action.

The Miguelense ceremonial pattern has been simplified by other processes more conscious and direct than fortuitous theft. Several communities have deliberately reduced both the number of ceremonial events they celebrate and the complexity of these events. Traditionally, each set of sponsors was responsible for a ceremonial round of three or four fiestas over the year. The image of aldea Subchal, for example, is the Virgen de Dolores, which was previously celebrated during Holy Week, on the day of Corpus Cristi, during the fiesta patronal, and on the day new cofrades were inaugrated. Under its new truncated arrangement, Subchal celebrates the saint's day only, and the amount spent is largely optional. Neither feast nor fireworks is required, but either may be arranged if the four cofrades care to meet the expense. The people expect only that a mass will be celebrated for their image.

Aldea Sícabe previously celebrated three fiestas per year but now observes only the feast day of its saint. Xponá also reduced its ceremonial round from three fiestas to one, for the same reason: "The people were spending much money—for this reason many did not want to be cofrade, because they would have to pay for three fiestas in the year." El Colmito had two fiestas each year, but about six years ago a catechist accepted the post and eliminated one of them because, he says, the aldea was spending too much *(por motivo que la aldea estaba haciendo mucho gasto).* As in Subchal, the amount spent is now up to the cofrades, a mass being the sole required expenditure.

The overall historical pattern of ritual breakdown in the aldeas of San Miguel has been for an administered, cost-sharing type of organization (in which two cofrades collect and disburse public funds) to intervene briefly between two sponsored types. In all aldeas where it has appeared, the succeeding sponsorship organization has been appended in number of sponsors and truncated in purpose and format compared to the traditional form. A similar pattern has been recorded in the Peruvian Indian community of Hualcán. In Hualcán, fiestas that were previously celebrated at different times of the year have been collapsed and are celebrated in common on the day of the patrona. There is less pomp and intricacy to the activities, and people complain of the costs. A Hualcaino says:

> In early times, we harvested a lot of things, like potatoes, corn, wheat, and barley. There was abundance. This is why they took the offices to give the fiestas of the Virgen del Perpetuo Socorro and Nuestro Señor Afligido. Now, when people plant and the fields do not yield much, they don't want to have these fiestas any more because potatoes and

wheat cost a lot. That is why they do not take the office of mayordomo any more. Now they just celebrate the fiesta of the Virgen Ursula, and they only have masses for the rest of the saints. They even used to celebrate the fiesta of the Virgen Ursula better (Stein 1961:253).

During the period in which the rules of public participation were being juggled and redefined, the people of San Miguel were attempting to preserve a delicate balance between the rate at which individuals would be taxed to support ceremonies and the equity with which the burden was distributed among community members. Simple, unvarnished economy was everywhere a basic issue; four communities went so far as to let their festive customs die rather than to continue paying the costs. Those aldeas that have maintained some public rituals have succeeded in doing so only by increasing the number of sponsors and reducing their responsibilities.

But felt costs were not the only factor in ceremonial modification. As felt costs were rising, the ceremonial inducement system was being weakened by social and political changes. Individuals were offered new reason for rejecting the folk religion and new means of avoiding traditional obligations.

The political changes initiated by the Revolution of 1944 largely disassociated power from ritual participation. Party politics rather than folk ritual service became the primary route to municipal office. Many men of local political importance have had no ritual service, and the municipio has even had one Protestant mayor. As men in the community became more confident in Spanish and more aware of their legal rights, it became more difficult for mayors to force cofradía participation. Mayors are no longer the isolated autocrats they were when the country was more primitive, communications less developed, and the Indian citizenry more ignorant of its fundamental rights. "There used to be more *respeto*," an old ex-mayor complained. "If you force people now, they run off to the *gobernación*." Now, conservative mayors will employ their moral authority on reluctant nominees, but they dare not use force. I once observed a mayor attempting to convince a young man who had been designated cofrade of San Miguel Arcángel to accept the post. He lectured him on the antiquity of the customs and on community spirit and duty, and urged him to come into his office for his *patente*, a document exempting him from all municipal taxes during his year in office. But he did not threaten him with jail.

The disassociation of power from ceremonial service had direct effects on the fiesta inducement system. Physical force was weakened and power was no longer a reward for ceremonial participation. In this sense, the motivating system in San Miguel became more like that of the communities of San Pedro Sacatepéquez, where people have always been closer to the protective office of the departmental governor and naked force has never been a factor in ceremonial participation. Men in Chamac and Petz laughed when I described the official coercion of Miguelense mayors. "If an authority ever tried that around here," one noted, "we would have *him* put in jail."

This sundering of the religious and political spheres of Miguelense life was made more complete with the arrival of missionary priests. Current missionaries always have outside sources of income, so they need not rely on the creation and maintenance of Indian rituals for their subsistence. Their central purpose is to "reconvert" the Indians, purifying their beliefs and activities in order to join them to the orthodox Church. This purpose puts contemporary priests in direct opposition to the entire folk-ritual complex.

The new priests, those who have worked throughout the highlands during the resurgence of missionization that began in the early 1950s, are vigorously opposed to folk ritual. They see themselves in competition with the chimanes for the loyalty and salvation of the people—a view the chimanes share. They object to profane use of religious objects in folk ritual, as well as to the doctrinal inaccuracy of the rituals themselves. They are shocked at the drunkenness, brawling, and sexual license that occur on supposedly holy days. And they consider the expenditures of the sponsors to be wasteful and damaging to the family.

In San Miguel, priests have moved against folk ceremonial organizations in various ways, some conscious, others not. They represent a new locus of authority and another line of defense against coercive mayors. Padre Cirpiano and his successors, considering the selection of cofrades to be church business, have opposed interference by civil officials. They have also established an official church policy on cofradía activity that stresses the central importance of masses in honor of the saints (a relatively inexpensive ritual element), declares feasting, fireworks, and secular music optional, and excessive drinking undesirable. This official position has lent ideological and authoritative support to people who would avoid or simplify ritual service.

Finally, in their reconversion efforts the missionaries, both Catholic and Protestant, have opened new social divisions that have weakened conservative social pressures in the municipio. Religious movements have established socio-religious communities within the municipio, communities that are tight, organized, largely endogamous, and in ideological competition with one another and with folk Catholicism. The religious objectives that individuals seek have diversified. Men now identify with their religious subgroup more than with the aldean and municipal communities, because it is this more limited group that satisfies so many of their needs, occupies so much of their time, and shares so many of their goals.

Subchal: A Close Look at a Miguelense Aldea

The economic difficulties the municipio has suffered, in conjunction with weakening of the traditional inducement system, have provided a motivational basis for simplification of communal ritual. We can clarify these processes through a closer look at the ritual history of aldea Subchal. This isolated hamlet is spread over a series of high ridges, with its closest border a 45-minute hike from the nearest road. Its residents have suffered the same economic misfortunes—intense population pressure, soil erosion, and spiraling involvement in goods and labor markets—as their neighbors in other aldeas. Their religious history has been particularly turbulent. Nearly half the hamlet has become involved in a strong catequista movement, and the community has appended and truncated its traditional fiesta. But some men, in opposition to the general trend, are presently attempting to initiate a new fiesta in honor of El Señor de Esquipulas, an image that Padre Cirpiano donated to their new aldean chapel a decade or so ago. The case of Subchal clearly exposes the interplay of costs, rewards, and ritual organization under conditions of declining income.

The hamlet has a long history of economically inspired resistance to cofradía service. The Virgen de Dolores, with its yearly cycle of four festivities, was a heavy burden. Ex-cofrades consistently estimate the sponsorship cost as around Q40 per sponsor in material expenditures, plus one to two weeks of ceremonial labor. Most cofrades raised the money on the fincas (almost all expenditures were in cash). An informant who financed his service in two seasons of harvest labor said his father had told him of a time when men sold animals to accumulate ceremonial reserves, but he himself knows of no such cases.

Cofrades, along with the aldean civil officials, were chosen each year in a hamlet meeting. The auxiliary mayor of the hamlet and his councilmen presided over the meeting and were among its most influential voices, but they did not autocratically appoint sponsors. Names would be suggested, excuses offered and debated, and a general consensus reached. After the group had decided on its representatives, however, the appointee was obligated to accept or face the municipal mayor. Only if he could find someone to take his place could he legitimately avoid service.

Along with the importance of power in the maintenance of the organization came its inevitable abuse. The pattern of ritual participation in Subchal was distorted compared to that of traditional Indian communities. The characteristic of generalized support for the fiesta system, with a few men eager to serve and a few others just as eager not to, did not exist in Subchal. No one volunteered to serve, and some people are still bitter that certain poor but docile men were badgered into serving more than once, while no member of the three wealthiest families in the aldea had ever served a cargo, because of their personal pull with municipal authorities. People report recent widespread cynicism and some outright belligerence toward the fiesta institution. Men of strong character (one informant referred to them as *los nerviosos*) had at times publicly refused to accept nomination to sponsorship, threatening to abandon their responsibility and spend the whole year working on the coast if their appointments were not withdrawn.

There was, however, a reservoir of sincere support for the cofradía de la Virgen within the community. Some men had great faith in the costumbres, and willingly upheld them. But the balance was tipped the other way, toward skepticism, reluctance, and rejection. "If they had not forced us," one man put it bluntly, "there would have been no fiesta for the Virgen." *Voluntad,* the spirit to sacrifice for the saints, was at low ebb.

When Chepe Aguilar was appointed to the cofradía in the early 1950s, he was one of the unwilling many. Though he had not yet converted to Catholicism and ideologically favored the fiesta sysem, the costs were so burdensome to him that he served only because of the threat of punishment. In those days, he says, he had to struggle to feed his family, so the extra cost of the cofradía was oppressive.

Toward the end of the decade, Chepe came under the influence of Padre Cipriano. Chepe has always been one of those rigidly principled individuals who resist any authoritative demand they consider unreasonable or unjust. He despises finca labor, which he managed to avoid even during the forced-work period of Ubico. He has also avoided the army, which regularly invades the Indian highlands to practice strong-arm "recruiting," and he was, as described earlier, a pioneer worker in Indian political organization during the brief decade of post-Revolution "libertad." This principled obstinence, coupled with his negative cofradía experience, led him to question the priest about the validity of the aldean ritual costumbres. In Chepe's words:

> Previously, the fiestas were organized around the costumbres of the indigenous people and run by the chimanes. They involved much drinking and fireworks, but the cofrades generally did not pay to have a mass celebrated. Padre Cipriano said, "This is not the way a cofradía should be. All your activities are very expensive, but they are all invalid; they are not agreeable to God. All the sacrificial turkeys, *copal,* drunkenness, spending of money, and marimbas. Why? All of this and the words of the chimanes are not heard by God."
>
> And he said, "Why are you buying meat? It is fine if you can afford it, but it is for this reason that the people do not want to serve as cofrade—because it is so costly (*porque dinero quiere*). And this money is going for nothing. For drunkenness and uproar. If he has money to spend, fine. But if not, he should pay for a mass only, for this money is not wasted. It is a sacrifice that God will reward with his benediction."
>
> Thus little by little we became catequistas, and little by little we lost all those customs, paying only for the mass.

Padre Cipriano told Chepe, in effect, that there were no religious reasons why a good Catholic should sponsor a traditional fiesta, and a number of reasons why he should not. He also told him that he would be Chepe's ally in any attempt to "purify" the aldea's practices.

Armed with these assurances, Chepe, his brother-in-law, and two other recent converts approached the aldean officials sometime around 1960 and requested the cofradía of the Virgen for the following year, to the official's delight. Once in office, they refused to accept any expense other than that of a mass on the day of the saint, an expenditure of Q8, which they divided among the four of them.

Some people were angry. Chepe's brother-in-law was at one point forced to flee a group of belligerent, drunk, conservative men. The chimanes were enraged, and there were rumors of plans to waylay Chepe and kill Padre Cipriano, though these never matured. In the following years, sometimes converts and sometimes men de costumbre would be appointed to the co-fradía, and fiesta expenditures varied accordingly. On occasion both converts and conservatives served together. Justo de Paz was nominated cofrade shortly after he converted, serving alongside three conservative men. These men chose to meet the full festive obligation and Justo did his full share, only refusing to contribute for liquor and for the fees of the chimán.

Converts, however, have gained complete control of the fiesta organization in recent years. From at least 1966 onward all cofrades have been converts and all fiestas have been served in the new way. As the number of converts grew, support for traditional religion declined. The number of chimanes diminished as fewer people engaged them for the ancient birth, harvest, death, and curing ceremonies. Chimán-financed ceremonials also declined. Chimanes traditionally celebrated a special fiesta every year, the fiesta de la Santa Cruz, which they paid for out of their earnings. This fiesta included feasting and music, just like a fiesta de cofradía, so in this way the fees chimanes earned for their ritual services were plowed back into conspicuous giving, rather than benefiting them personally. There would sometimes be as many as ten fiestas de la Santa Cruz in Subchal every May, staged by as many chimanes. In 1969 only three chimanes celebrated this ritual.

Once the costs of sponsorship were reduced to an acceptable level, however, and the organization was once again in the control of a face-to-face, sacred community, the old structure of fiesta voluntad reemerged among the Catholics of Subchal. Catholic converts form a cohesive group that collectively admires the mass, the patron saint, and service to the saint. Devout men regularly express their support for the new fiesta, and nominations are no longer fraught with strife and controversy. More significant, at least five men have served as sponsor of the new fiesta more than once, one of these having served three times.

A tendency toward overparticipation by the relatively wealthy is also reemerging in Subchal. The man who has served three times is Anacleto Diaz, the smuggler so admired for the wealth he accumulated despite adverse beginnings. Anacelto has actually served four sponsorships, the first taking place before Chepe provided the new format. His first service was against his will. There was no voluntad in those days, he says, "because of the money. But now one doesn't spend as much." Other men in the aldea have made virtually identical assessments of the effect of the decrease in costs: "Before, the costs came from finca work, and for this reason the people did not like to accept. Now, an expenditure of Q2 for the whole year is nothing."

During the year of his first cofradía service, Anacleto converted to Catholicism and dedicated himself to his new religion and co-religionists. Besides cofradía services, he has attended two cursillos and plans to add another as soon as he finds time. He owns one of the finest houses in the aldea (his kitchen is more substantial than some people's houses) but he plans to improve it with a concrete floor and an additional room in order to have more space to host neighborhood religious meetings. For Anacleto, conspicuous giving is not restricted to ceremonial sponsorship.

Chepe Aguilar is another of the wealthier men who has been a conspicuous overparticipator in new Catholic activities, cofradía and otherwise. He has been to several cursillos, served as senior brother of Subchal for several years and as president of one of the Church committees. Despite his antagonism toward the old fiestas, Chepe is now the major force behind recent attempts to establish a cofradía of El Señor de Esquipulas. In 1969, Chepe, as first cofrade, initiated a fiesta for this saint. His celebration was slightly more opulent than the new fiestas for the Virgen. Four cofrades paid for two masses, food for the priest and aldean officials, a small quantity of fireworks, and a marimba for public dancing. Their total expenditure was Q59. Otherwise, the event was identical to the new fiestas that have appeared in Subchal and elsewhere. Financing was based on multiple sponsorship, participation was voluntary, and the amount spent optional. The event began and ended in a single 24-hour period, and the cofrades attempted to maintain an orthodox, solemn tone by making the mass the focal point and refusing to supply liquor to the spectators.

The future of this new cofradía is problematic. Chepe is especially devoted to the image of El Señor de Esquipulas because it was donated by his beloved Padre Cipriano shortly before the priest's tragic death. Others are less interested. There were complaints, after the event, about the "uproar" and drunkenness (privately financed) of some of those who attended. After the fiesta Chepe searched diligently for men willing to serve the following year, under the priest's strict orders that he in no way attempt to influence their acceptance. He found no takers. When I left the field he had given up, saying that if no one volunteered, he would celebrate the fiesta again himself in four or five years.

TWELVE

Fiesta Reorganization in the San Pedro Region

This chapter considers the fate of the fiesta system at the other end of the economic spectrum, where peasant communties are establishing themselves as modern participants in the national economy and society.

Reorganization in the Cabecera

Before recent changes, the people of San Pedro organized their public ceremonies through cofradías and comités. Cofradías were responsible for the religious aspects of fiestas, and were based on the principle of conspicuous giving. Comités organized secular activities—soccer games, carnivals, social dances, and the crowning of queens—spending monies from taxes or public collections. Today, fiesta committees are sometimes associated with municipal government, sometimes not. Since the fiesta of San Pedro, patron saint of the township, is an important commercial event, the municipal fiesta committee has always spent considerable sums from the town treasury on its preparation. In some aldeas, public officials play a similar organizing role. New fiesta committees, however—those recently set up in many town cantones and some hamlets—are invariably composed of independent groups of interested Catholics. This tendency represents the inevitable splitting off of government from religion as a community becomes religiously diversified. Protestants are now numerous and powerful in San Pedro, so Catholics must shoulder their own ritual responsibilities.

, In the parochial archives, the earliest document with information on ritual organization is dated May 5, 1786. It lists, on the occasion of a visit of the archbishop of Quezaltenango, the nine ceremonial organizations of San

Pedro, along with their holdings. Of the modern cofradías only Jesús Nazareno, the Virgin de Dolores, and the Virgen de Mercedes are on this list. It appears that traditional ritual is not as stable as we often think. Since the end of the eighteenth century, this document implies, San Pedranos have modified their pantheon and ritual calendar considerably, eliminating or deemphasizing nine major images and adding three others. Even the present municipal patron is not on the 1786 list.[1]

We should expect, therefore, that any "traditional" ritual system will fluctuate in form as certain activities or gods gain or lose importance in the community eye. People are fickle, even with their deities. The changes that have been occurring in the town over the last two decades, however, are of a different order. Compared to languid traditional fluctuation, these have been rapid, dramatic, and complete. Two previously prestigious cofradías (Corpus Cristi and Virgen de Mercedes) have virtually disappeared, and many others have been reorganized into comités or orthodox hermandades. Recently, San Pedranos have not simply added and subtracted events within a given organizational format, but have been elaborating new kinds of organization.

The direction of ritual changes in the town has been toward the ceremonial forms of urban Ladinos in Guatemala City, Antigua, and Quezaltenango. Gone are the unorthodox and "undignified" prankster dances and the celebration of Judas. Individuals are freer to join and leave religious organizations, or even to reject ceremonial participation altogether. At present, most festivities are administered, rather than sponsored, the major ones by large, permanent-membership voluntary organizations, and the others by small *ad hoc* committees. Ceremonial activity is also largely concentrated now in Holy Week, a pattern which coincides with that of the larger Guatemalan cities. On the municipal level, in fact, Holy Week activities have become more elaborate over the last 20 years, during which time two of the three major municipal cofradías not associated with Easter have degenerated.

Most of these changes occurred in the 1950s and early 1960s. The *asociación* that celebrates Sagrado Corazón de Jesús was formed in 1950, the hermandad of El Señor Sepultado in 1953. The last cofradía fiesta for the municipal patron was in 1960, with the hermandad being formed the subsequent year. The newest municipal hermandad (Jesús de la Humildad) was organized in 1963, the single cantón hermandad in 1965.

Ceremonial financing is now arranged almost exclusively through dues, public collections, and fund-raising events, so drains on the time and wealth of individual people have been greatly reduced. El Señor Sepultado was the first town cofradía to be reorganized into a hermandad, and it is interesting to compare the distribution of costs of this event under the two ceremonial forms. The traditional cofradía held its major activities on Saturday of Holy Week, but preparations in the house of the mayordomo began more than a week earlier. The mayordomo's family made candles and several hundred pounds of bread, cleaned and whitewashed the house, and dispatched men to the coast to fetch four quintals of fruit and flowers to adorn the saint. During Holy Week the mayordomo and his family hosted one all-night vigil, attended three masses, and participated in two processions—one of which was so intricate that it lasted five hours. The family also fed the devotos who assisted them through the week, and prepared two formal meals for 30 or more people. The cofrade's commitment and obligations were obviously large. The last man to hold this position before the reorganization estimates that the event cost his household around Q90, plus 10 days' labor.

Today, the hermandad of El Señor Sepultado spends some Q200 on Holy Week activities, but the costs are distributed among its 120 members. Rarely does a member contribute more than a quetzal or two per year. Labor costs are equally dispersed. Members are required to attend a mass and procession on Holy Friday, and to serve occasionally as treasurer or secretary, or hold some other office in hermandad administration. This reduction in individual burden is the single most outstanding feature of the new ceremonial organizations. Whether the event is a major one such as the above, or a minor neighborhood fiesta organized by a small committee of dedicated people, no one is required to donate large amounts of time or to spend deeply from personal savings to stage the event.

Ceremonial reorganization in San Pedro's cantones has followed these same lines, except that the new organizations are smaller, less elaborate, and less sacred. In some cases these neighborhood committees have been formed specifically to supplant cofradías; in other cases they coexisted with cofradías, and expanded their activities at the cofradías' demise. In cantón San Juan de Dios, a cofrade was previously responsible for the entire fiesta. In 1961 a comité was formed to reconstruct the neighborhood's earthquake-destroyed chapel and to elaborate the annual festivity. This was the first year that the fiesta was secularized by the addition of games and dances to its regular ritual activities. Since 1961, people have requested the cofradía for all but two years. When no one volunteers, the committee organizes a vigil and novena, financed out of public collections. Cantones Santa Maria and San Augustín also formed comittees, originally to repair earthquake-damaged chapels, and subsequently elaborated them as they lost their cofradías.

Outside Influences

The history of ritual reinstitutionalization in San Pedro has been quite different from what it was in San Miguel Ixtahuacán. The various ideas for coping with ritual problems in San Miguel seem to have come out of the community itself, as local solutions to local problems. Ceremonial organization in that township, though far different from what it was, has not taken national form. But ritual behavior in San Pedro is becoming ever more consistent with that of major Ladino towns, which implies a diffusion of ideas.

This diffusion has definitely occurred, as several cases indicate. Around 1935, a man from aldea Mávil accepted the town cofradía of El Señor Sepultado, and stored the ritual goods in the house of a townsman named Apolinario Velásquez. When Holy Week approached, the designate failed to take up his obligation, so Apolinario decided to serve the image himself. He continued this service for the following 15 years. (It was not unusual for men to serve Holy Week images for a number of years consecutively.) In the beginning, Apolinario served with voluntad, but 15 years is a long time. Toward the end of his term he regularly searched for a replacement; no one would accept the obligation. His devotos, furthermore, the men who had previously assisted him in his office, began to withdraw their support in the final years.

By the early 1950s the celebration of this saint was in serious difficulty. The costs were more than one family could bear year after year (Apolinario, to make his situation worse, had recently lost his wife), and public support was weak. About this time Apolinario had the good fortune to meet Humberto Santizo, a Quezalteco residing in San Pedro. Humberto is a Ladino and a devout Catholic whose family has long been active in hermandad affairs in other communities. Around 1918 his father and grandfather founded the first hermandad in the town of San Cristóbal Totonicapán, and an uncle subsequently participated in the organization of the hermandad of El Señor Sepultado de San Nicolás, now the largest brotherhood in Quezaltenango. Humberto, aware of Apolinario's dilemma, urged him to found an hermandad. With the help of Humberto, a small group of citizens, and the parish priest—who offered his total cooperation—Apolinario did just that. The hermandad quickly swelled to 180 members, and, though it has since lost some members, it is still one of the strongest hermandades in San Pedro.

Although El Señor Sepultado was the first formal hermandad, it was not the first administered ritual organization founded in San Pedro. Three years earlier, the minor cofradía of Sagrado Corazón de Jesús had been reestablished as an "asociación." The process of reorganization of this fiesta was very similar to that of El Señor Sepultado. The image of Sagrado Corazón de Jesús was originally owned by a wealthy woman who sponsored its fiesta every year. At her death it passed to a succession of other women, and finally to a comerciante named Mariano Joachin, who served as cofrade throughout the 1940s. The cofradía's activities, which took place during Holy Week and on the saint's day in August, were financed by the cofrade himself, and from small donations he solicitated.

Mariano began serving out of *devoción* but, as Apolinario had, he encountered declining support. Not only could he find no one to replace him, but people refused to help him with expenses. One woman from whom he had requested a donation of candles told him flatly that if he couldn't afford the post he should not have accepted it, which so dismayed him that he began paying all costs personally.

In 1949 Mariano discussed his problem with his friend Bonifacio Miranda, who had been working as an agricultural extension agent in various highland municipios. Bonifacio was impressed with the power and value of committees, which he was promoting everywhere to stimulate agricultural improvement. He was struck with the idea that a committee could produce greater support for Mariano's fiesta: "I thought it would be a better form", Bonifacio explained. "It would reduce the costs of the single individual, perhaps amplify the festivities, and would allow more people to participate."

This idea was a practical inspiration on the part of Bonifacio, who is not a religious man. In this respect he differs from the religiously experienced Humberto Santizo. But the two are similar in that both are men of broad outside experience, familiar with new systems of potential benefit to their home pueblo. Shortly after his conversation with Bonifacio, Mariano was advised by yet another outsider, a young man from Zacapa working in the San Pedro church, about forming the new organization along appropriate Catholic lines, and the asociación was created.

Organizational changes in the cofradías of El Señor Sepultado and Sagrado Corazón were similar, since in both cases reorganization was prompted by the ideas of men of broad outside experience. The two cases are also similar in that each fiesta experienced a period of declining support prior to reorganization, during which time conservative men attempted, almost alone, to save it. The same has occurred in virtually all other cases. As the community modernized, it factionalized. Previously latent feelings of religious disinterest intensified and spread, until those of such persuasion felt strong enough to reject publicly the obligations of cofrades. The remaining conservatives then made noble efforts to save the ancient customs, finally yielding to the new wave and rescuing the event with the help of experienced people.

When it becomes clear that the traditional organization is failing, conservatives and progressives often join in curious cooperation to save the event. Men like Bonifacio and Humberto had little in common with the old Indian cofrades they helped. When the fiesta patronal of San Pedro Apóstol was being reorganized, traditional and progressive elements came together in one man named Sebastián Gonsález. The fiesta of San Pedro, in its religious element, had suffered "years in which it had been decaying." The 1960 cofrade was the last; searching the town and the aldeas, he found no one who would take over the post. Sebastián Gonsález finally agreed to take charge if he would be allowed to make certain changes in the staging of the rituals.

Sebastián is an agressive, dynamic man, and a successful entrepreneur. He began life as a muleteer, but moved into trucking as the transport business grew. He once owned a considerable coffee finca in the Zona Reina, and now as an old man supports himself from a 500-cuerda wheat farm in nearby San Lorenzo. His family carries on his entrepreneurial spirit. His daughter (killed in a truck accident during my stay) was one of the principal transportistas of San Pedro; his son runs a daily bus to Quezaltenango.

Despite his worldly experiences, Sebastián is a devout man who identifies strongly with the local saints. He has served several cofradías, including the cofradía of San Pedro in 1959. When he agreed to serve San Pedro again, it was for the second time in just a few years. Sebastián called together a small group of interested men and detailed the expenditures he had made as cofrade of San Pedro. Because of the exorbitant cost of sponsorship, he explained, willing cofrades could not longer be found. He suggested that the group could save the customs by forming an hermandad, such as those already operating in San Pedro[2] and those he knew from his travels around the country. The hermandad of San Pedro Apóstol was thus established.

The hermandad of San Pedro has never enjoyed the popularity of the big Holy Week brotherhoods. Too small to generate internal revenue, it relies on attracting donations from wealthy people to pay for masses, decoration of the anda and altar, music for the procession, and other ritual items. The small

Holy Week hermandad of Jesús de la Humildad finances its activities in precisely the same way, listing contributors in its festive bulletin along with the item each supplied. These hermandades seem to be intermediate forms between true cofradías on the one hand and true hermandades and comités on the other. They provide opportunities for significant giving (the *misa mayor* of the fiesta of San Pedro Apóstol costs its devoto Q80), as well as social recognition for this giving. But it is, compared to the responsibilities of traditional cofrades, an attenuated and diffused form of giving.

The hermandad of San Pedro Apóstol is presently doing poorly. It was founded by about 14 men, all of them heavily involved with the town saints. Two of these men had previously been cofrades of San Pedro, another had served both San Pedro and Corpus Cristi, and one other had volunteered as celebrant of the anda for the fiesta of San Pedro when the cofradía folded. The organization has not attracted new members, however, and even the old ones seem to be losing interest. For the last six years, the presidency of the brotherhood has been held by a single man, who can find no one interested in taking over. He says he will continue as long as he is able to preserve the customs, but he is pessimistic about the future.

The fiesta of San Pedro Apóstol is in no danger of disappearing—it is commercially much too important for that to be allowed. Its traditional religious element, however, is in jeopardy. This fiesta is changing its form from a sacred event with economic attributes to a commercial and recreational festivity, or from Holy Day to Holiday, as Redfield labeled a similar trend in Yucatan. The evaporating significance of this particular ritual indicates that administered organizations are not a panacea for cofradía collapse, and also that the fluctuating popularity of deities continues even with modernized ceremonial forms. Holy Week saints are now in vogue, and increasingly monopolize the town's ritual energy.

Economic Development and Ritual Motivation

New ideas spread in the manner of diseases. For them to successfully infect a new population, there must be both exposure and susceptibility. Recently, the town of San Pedro has become ever more exposed to new ideas. So, to a great degree, have its adjacent aldeas and, to a lesser degree, its remote aldeas. But contagion will not allow an idea to spread and flourish unless the exposed population is susceptible to its influence. The case of Petz demonstrates this. In Petz, a resident explained, when a fiesta lacks a sponsor the "hermandad" will carry the saint procession. This hermandad is not a "true hermandad like in San Pedro," he went on, but merely the aldean Acción Católica. The people of Petz are thus aware of administered ceremonial organizations, but they have not developed such organizations. Within their community the idea is nonviable.

In this section we turn from questions of exposure to those of susceptibility. Ideas for reformulating public ceremonies along national lines drifted into San Pedro with men experienced in the national culture. The ideas are now spreading to outlying hamlets through normal channels of community interaction. Why have these ideas been strongly infectious in some places, inactive in others?

The answer is laid bare by the distribution of communities in which administered organizations have been or are being established—by the epidemiological boundary of the idea. It is the more modern communities of the township that have embraced the new idea. San Pedro itself, the most modern of these communities, has embraced it the longest and most intimately. People become more susceptible to ritual change as they become economically and socially progressive. Development in San Pedro has disrupted the balance between felt costs and felt rewards that supported conspicuous giving, just as poverty has in San Miguel Ixtahuacán. The reasons, however, are much more complex in the San Pedro case, and the processes of change more numerous and intertwined. It is helpful to begin by looking at ritual breakdown in aldeas Chamac and San José Caben. Situated on the outskirts of the town, these aldeas are presently experiencing the kinds of economic and ritual change that began in the town years ago.

"Accepting the cofradía is just like buying a knitting machine on time," a conservative woman from Chamac explains. "You have got to save your pennies." As economies develop and knitting machines and other desirable gadgetry become abundant, people must begin choosing between hoarding pennies for the saint or for the gadgetry—a battle the saint inevitably loses. The woman herself rejects this truth. She recently salvaged the faltering cofradía of San Isidro Chamac by volunteering for a second sponsorship. This piety stirred a conservative reaction in the hamlet which may keep the organization going for a while longer. But as more and more Chamaquenses opt for education, entrepreneurship, and consumerism, San Isidro's feast will change; of this there is no doubt.

Eugenio Monzón of San José Caben is presently feeling the effect of these economic pressures. As a young man, Eugenio served the image of El

Señor Sepultado in his aldea. He served voluntarily, and still believes that mayordomía is a legitimate religious sacrifice. I talked with him in 1970, only days after he received a petition from the hamlet comité católico to serve the failing image of San José, the aldean patron, in the coming year. Despite his devotion and financial capability, Eugenio had decided to decline. "If it had been last year, I would have accepted," he said. Now he was saving to build a better house. He had already purchased the lumber and planned to install a cooking griddle and hot water bath, so his house would be as nice as the two or three other "modern" residences recently constructed in the hamlet. Eugenio's present house, with its privy and open cook-fire, would have satisfied his father. Had it satisfied Eugenio, too, the cofradía of San José would be in less jeopardy. It is unlikely that Eugenio will ever again support the fiesta system. His two sons are weaving to finance the higher education they desperately desire. Eugenio plans to aid them, which will consume his extra pennies for years to come.

Eugenio's case dramatizes the immediate impact on cofradía membership of rising desires to invest and consume. It also indicates how far these desires have spread down the social order in San Pedro Sacatepéquez. Eugenio is a campesino who lives by planting corn and vegetables and traveling the mountains and coast to buy pigs for a local butcher. He lives comfortably but is by no means wealthy or entrepreneurial. He is also an uneducated, rustic folk-Catholic. New aspirations, nevertheless, for both himself and his children, are strongly implanted and increasingly influence his economic behavior.

Local people recognize the rising opportunity costs of sponsorship: "Now our costs are greater. If one has children he must put them in the *colegio*. This costs money and previously it wasn't done." On the community level, the cases of aldea Chamac and the boca costa municipio of El Quetzal show that new economic opportunities can weaken the fiesta system in several ways. Ceremonial voluntad is wavering in Chamac. Masked dances were given up at least 15 years ago. The cofradía of San Isidro, the aldean patron, almost failed in the early 1960s, and the conservative movement now upholding it seems foredoomed. The fiesta has become highly secularized, with games and social dancing. In 1970 some people were talking of organizing a children's group to stage a masked dance the following year, which would transform a meaningful adult custom into a simple diversion.

Interest in fiesta sponsorship has declined even further in El Quetzal. In the early 1960s the cofradía of the municipal patron was abandoned with apparent finality. El Quetzal, on the whole, is a less prosperous community than Chamac, and one in which new socioeconomic opportunities are more restricted. The community is ethnically mixed; some of its residents are Ladinos, others are Indian migrants from the highlands. Much of the local land is tied up in enormous absentee-owned coffee plantations, and most residents are either small landholders or permanent finca workers. Neither group is economically progressive. There is, however, a small entrepreneurial bourgeoisie in the township center that supports itself with small stores, by purchasing coffee futures, by making loans against the harvests of small holders, and by accumulating land. These people are expansive petty capitalists. Of the five wealthiest families, four have land, deal in coffee, and own stores. The other is a landholder. All have educated children who have left the community.

The cofradía of the municipal patron collapsed in El Quetzal because of the anger these wealthy people generated by refusing to accept sponsorship. (Informants in San Pedro say the fiesta of their patron collapsed, in part, for the same reason: Why, people thought, should we serve when those so much more able refuse?) In El Quetzal the critical straw was added when a wealthy man finally accepted the cargo and discharged it perfunctorily. He refused to hire a marimba, and rather than serving the food in the familial atmosphere of his home, dispatched it to the church. The community withdrew in disgust. In 1964 two young men attempted, as one of them said, "to put the customs en marcha again," but without success. They volunteered for the cofradía and staged a traditional fiesta, but when they searched the town for replacements, no one would accept.

Elite withdrawal has caused resentment in Chamac as well. Chamac is made up of a small number of textile merchants and truckers who are as wealthy as any in the township, a large middle group of peasant farmers and craftsmen who live comfortably but not expansively, and a few poor families. Nowadays cofrades invariably come from the middle group.[3] "The pobres would like to serve but are not able; the ricos can, but refuse," one resident put it. Of the six wealthiest men in Chamac, only one has served in the aldea's fiesta system, and he is the oldest of the group.

Compared to El Quetzal, however, Chamac is a more stable, religious community, with a stronger sense of long-standing custom. The greater income of its middle group also renders ritual conservatism easier. Most of the middle group in Chamac have sound and independent household economies that provide them comfortable subsistence but no riches. The two people most directly responsible for recently saving Chamac's cofradía are both older, prosperous campesinos who produce surpluses in grain and milk. One has a large garden as well, and the other makes weekly selling trips to the coast. A neighbor says of them: "They want to develop like a tree, covering more and more land. All they want is land. Other things don't interest them."

Progress continues to penetrate the middle group, however, especially through the youth. One young Chamaquense has already earned a professional degree. Ten others are enrolled in secondary school, and many more are pressuring their parents for educational support. These young people have a new, nonpeasant orientation to life, which entails new goals and costs. As they pursue these goals in increasing numbers, fiesta support will wither and the aldean cofradía will either change or die. When new economic opportunities are restricted to a small segment of the community, as they are in El Quetzal, conspicuous giving can collapse out of general resentment over elite withdrawal. In a community such as Chamac, where opportunities are opening on a broader front, community polarization is less extreme and communal ritual suffers more from new desires than from new rancors.

Its also interesting that in neither case did more than a fraction of the community become affected by modern impulses before the fiesta system was seriously weakened. When people begin to withdraw, for whatever reason, it has the double effect of reducing the esteem sponsors earn while transferring the costs of sponsorship to a smaller group. Some of those who withdraw make things even worse by actively criticizing the fiestas and attempting to dissuade others from serving. When this occurs, people begin to feel damned if they do, damned if they don't, and ritual spending becomes harder to rationalize on any level.

A mayordomo's tragedy in Chamac reveals that many people of that hamlet are now caught squarely in such a dilemma. In 1969 this unfortunate man was cleaning and decorating for his fiesta when two of his children mysteriously died. Some people interpreted this as evidence for the power of the saint, who was punishing the sponsor for accepting the cargo in bad faith. Others said it just shows how pointless fiestas are. This event prompted me to discuss the validity of fiesta sponsorship with over 30 men in Chamac and San José Caben. I discovered an atmosphere of questioning and doubt. In San José only one man felt that traditional sponsorship was a valid religious obligation. In Chamac, five were so inclined. The rest were surprisingly skeptical, defending themselves with everything from orthodox Christian arguments to militant atheism: "Superstition!" "It is a lie. From what little I know, those *ídolos* are not miraculous.'' ''These expenses bring no profit whatsoever, over the body, the soul, or the economic situation.''

Belief in the saints' power to punish is also fading. One man was so lacking in awe that he even poked fun at the village patron: ''Perhaps a miraculous saint could do us harm, but this fellow we have here doesn't do anything.'' And the idea that fiesta sponsorship is meaningless to God—the teaching Padre Cipriano worked so hard to implant in the hidden villages of San Miguel—is broadly and spontaneously accepted in these more progressive locales.

Such a period of skepticism, during which the community loses its focused, folk-Catholic religiousness, generally precedes the actual reorganization of ritual. The pattern of elite withdrawal in Chamac and El Quetzal implies that new economic motives are strong contributors to this skepticism. The social changes that accompany economic development, especially growing contact with nonlocal people and associated sensitivity to national cultural standards, also increase resistance and doubt. Entrepreneurial men tend to withdraw from the fiesta system not only because they have more to lose economically, but also because, like the young students, they have less to gain socially. Much more than peasants, their work takes them outside the community, where they develop new associates. ''The ricos have no love for the aldea,'' one Chamaquense complained, ''because they have their friends in other places.''

The pressures currently threatening traditional rituals in Chamac and San José Caben developed much earlier in San Pedro itself. National standards of appropriate ritual behavior began finding their way to San Pedro as early as 1927, when Claudio Miranda was municipal mayor. At that time the fiesta of Corpus Cristi was enlivened by the antics of costumed pranksters who danced, mocked people, leaped in public fountains, and created general uproar. After years of studying law in Guatemala City, Claudio found these activities ''antisocial,'' and officially prohibited the custom. ''There are some things that are out of place in a civilized pueblo,'' he explained. ''These things must be eliminated.''

In the 1950s Bernardo Soto outlawed the Judas fiesta for similar reasons. The Holy Week hanging and burying of the Judas effigy was profaned in San Pedro by ribaldry, drunkenness, and uncontrolled adolescent excitement. It contrasted blatantly with the solemnity of other Holy Week events, and often interfered with them. In the early 1950s two sophisticated and very Catholic young women from Guatemala City visited Bernardo Soto for Holy Week. He still remembers their horror at the Judas spectacle, and his chagrin that his community still engaged in such backward customs.

"*¡Qué barbaridad, don Bernardo!*" they said to me. "We thought this was a town of culture, of religion and respect. How can this happen?" And this made me feel ashamed, because they came from the capital, a very cultured city. It was then that I began to notice these anomalies.

As mayor, Bernardo initiated action against the custom, which was soon discontinued.

Since Claudio Miranda's early attack on native rituals, San Pedro's accelerating modernization has left it increasingly susceptible to national religious standards. Political modernization seems to have played little role here, since politics and religion have long been separated in San Pedro. Unlike the situation in San Miguel Ixtahuacán, fiesta motivation in San Pedro has apparently always been voluntary. Disruption of this voluntary motivation has come largely from economic development and the social changes accompanying it.

Commercial elaboration and the development of white-collar occupations have presented San Pedranos with a multitude of new economic opportunities that compete directly with religious expenditure. Education, new material capital and consumer items, plus the diferentiation of labor in San Pedro's small firms have also generated many new nonreligious sources of prestige. The town's agricultural sector is still stagnant, and is also a continuing source of religious conservatism, but San Pedro has moved a long way from the generalized, domestic self-sufficiency of its peasant past. The capitalist entrepreneurs are often openly hostile to the fiesta system, perhaps because of their high involvement with the new economy. Anselmo Orozco, for example, had the strange good fortune of being too poor to be a peasant, which forced him into the commercial occupations that made him rich. Because of his wealth—not despite it—he spurns fiesta sponsorship:

These people throw the house out the window! I prefer to save. When you have saved Q200 you imagine what it would be like to have Q500. When you have Q500 you want Q1000. It is better to have a bank account. The object is to rise. To buy things.

San Pedro's development, however, has not been restricted to a small elite. The general pattern of change going on in Chamac today has been developing in San Pedro for decades. Educational and occupational opportunities have expanded and modern aspirations have spread far down the economic ladder. A strong emulation effect, by pulling more and more people into this modern milieu, has promoted general skepticism of the native religion. External social relations, by growing away from the insular, defensive peasant type, have also affected fiestero motivation. Commerce, literacy, and modern occupations have carried San Pedranos into the outside world, creating new, external peer groups and tying the community to others with a complex of economic, kinship, and friendship bonds. San Pedro as a local community thus cannot sanction and reward communal spending as strongly as it could when it was a closed society.

The growth of external social relationships has also influenced the character of ritual giving, when it still occurs. Marta Orozco recently sponsored a fiesta for the patron saint of her neighborhood. Though motivated by a religious vow, her fiesta had many aspects of a private social affair. Attendance was by printed invitation only, a marimba orchestra was hired for formal dancing, and many of the guests were from out of town, some from Guatemala City.

Apolinario Velásquez, Mariano Joachin, and other old San Pedro cofrades were experiencing public cynicism and lack of support several decades before these appeared in Chamac and San José Caben. As economic and social change accelerated through the 1950s and 1960s, San Pedro's fiesta system was replaced by new ritual forms more appropriately modern and less burdensome to the individual. The speedy demise of the town's fiesta systems was thus matched and caused by its development. These changes have occurred so rapidly they have left in their wake a shrinking band of outraged old men. Unable to cope with the speed of events, these old conservatives are tragic residue of modernization, who find their only solace in stories of comrades who have "died" and been returned to life. Entering heaven, the stories go, these people are able to identify the saints from their long association with the images. God then returns them their life so they can guide the pueblo back to its true costumbres. These poignant, miraculous stories are common today in San Pedro; two old men told me they had had the experience themselves.

Notes

[1] Of the current San Pedro cofradías, only those of the Virgen de Dolores, Jesús Nazareno, and the Virgen de Mercedes are on the 1786 list. The Virgen de Mercedes was the original patrona of the community; from its inception in 1695 until 1829, the San Pedro parish was run by Mercedarian priests.

[2]The administred organizations that had already been founded in San Pedro when the cofradía of San Pedro Apóstol was reorganized where the Asociación del Sagrado Corazón de Jesús (established in 1950) and the hermandades of El Señor Sepultado (1953) and Jesús Nazereno (1955).

[3]I investigated the economic histories of 17 men who had served as cofrade or celebrant of the anda for the fiesta of San Isidro in Chamac. Sixteen of these men were campesinos, some of whom also engaged in weaving, carpentry, brickmaking, or peddling as secondary occupations. The single entrepreneur who had participated in fiesta sponsorship was a trucker and large landholder.

Local people are quite aware of the conspicuous nonparticipation of the wealthy and entrepreneurial men. One informant said: "The ricos are more resistant *(más duros)* than we are. What they want is to rise. They only spend their money on things which carry interest; they do not involve themselves in the cofradías. All they want is to invest their money—to buy merchandise and sell it elsewhere. But money spent on an image, this money does not return, and this is what they do not want."

THIRTEEN

Ritual Stability in Petz and Cucho

The relative stability of native ritual life in San Pedro Petz and San Cristóbal Cucho has two possible causes. The economic situation of these villages, for one, favors ritual consumption. Petz and Cucho are not heavily proletarian, like San Miguel, nor are they modernizing, like San Pedro. Because their lives focus strongly on the local community, sponsoring fiestas is still feasible for people in these villages.

Petz and Cucho also differ from the other communities I have studied in that neither has been exposed to vigorous missionization. French Canadian missionaries stationed in El Quetzal were just beginning to work in Cucho when I was in the field. Petz is rarely visited by a priest, and few people in either village are involved in orthodox religion. This lack of religious alternatives and pressures is another factor that may contribute to the folk-Catholic conservatism of these outlying locales.

Although in the absence of mission activity may be significant, in viewing rural Guatemala as a whole I think it is less important than the economic factor. Contemporary priests in San Pedro, for example, have facilitated the ceremonial reorganization of that community. Padre Aurelio, who helped found the earliest hermandades in San Pedro, was an effective, aggressive missionary who also formed the first local Acción Católica as well as the extremely devout lay organization called La Tercera Orden Franciscana. But San Pedro is an ancient parish whose faded records reveal that it has had a priest in residence continually since 1695. The community had 56 Catholic pastors before Padre Aurelio. Surely one of them was equally dedicated and charismatic, and could have purified Indian ritual if vigorous missionary effort were the crucial factor. The fiesta systems of Chamac and El Quetzal, we should also recall, have been upset by socioeconomic factors alone, without priestly interference.

In some cases, furthermore, Indian cults have resisted even the direct attacks of overzealous priests. The most famous case of missionary rejection is recorded in Mendelsohn's intriguing chapter on "The Scandals of Maximón" (1957). Santiago Atitlán, a municipio on Lake Atitlán, has always been a staunchly conservative Indian community. One of its major deities is the Maximón, a Judas effigy, which the Indians believe is especially powerful. He is indeed powerful enough to stir the wrath of clerics. Mendelsohn quotes Lothrop on an incident that occurred around 1914 (1957:368):

> About fifteen years ago a Bishop arrived in Atitlán for Holy Week and was duly horrified to discover his flock worshiping an image of Judas. He thereupon issued orders that the figure be burned. But before this could be done the people assembled in great numbers, armed with clubs and machetes, and shortly the bishop had to flee from the town with a mob of enraged Indians howling at his heels.

Mendelsohn himself observed the aftermath of a similar confrontation in 1950. A certain Padre Recinos who had been visiting Santiago from his base in a nearby town, arrived on Holy Wednesday of that year to suppress the cult of Maximón. Although he was warned that rash action would place him in danger, he kicked over part of the altar dressing of the image. According to a contemporary report:

> People got extremely angry and were about to set about killing the priest so someone fetched the literate boys and they were told to warn the priest to leave Maximón alone, for he was their god, and that he would go mad and die. The priest answered that he did not give a fig about going mad, but that he would not allow them to worship the man who had been Christ's worst enemy before the crucifixion. The people's temper got considerably worse and some shouted that he should be put to death because he wasn't a Catholic but a Protestant. The priest ran over to the convent to get his pistol and made as if to shoot the people, shouting "I die for the truth but let's see that you go too, and to hell for a pack of idolators and savages that you are!" But when the priest went back to the convent, then the people set up the stones again and placed Maximón there with a golden incense-burner, litres of aguardiente and especially thick candles. When the priest came out he kicked the incense-burner and candles, but as he held his pistol the guardians endured this without moving (Mendelsohn 1957:332).

In 1950 the villagers were less aggressive than they had been in 1914, and the ire of the people, though strong, produced no violence. (The priest, besides, had a pistol.) The community nevertheless clung to the worship of Maximón in the face of continued depredations by Recinos. Shortly after the Holy Week episode of 1950, Recinos returned unannounced to the village and stole two of the masks of the image. One of these he burned; the other, badly damaged, is now in a French museum. Conservative Indians went so far as to petition the government to intercede in their behalf. The cult soon resumed normal practices, and is still in operation despite continued missionary activity.

Padre Recinos had formed a small group of converts in his years of work in Santiago, but his progress was slow, perhaps goading him to dramatic and dangerous action. His lack of progress was because people had little interest in his message; by and large they were content with their traditional gods and rituals. As an instructive comparison, it was just four years after the Recinos conflict in Santiago that mayor Bernardo Soto prohibited the celebration of Judas in San Pedro. Though this embittered some people, the community as a whole was hardly aroused. San Pedro had already begun to modernize and turn away from its native cults for social and economic reasons. Within two or three years of Soto's action the celebration of Judas in San Pedro was extinct.

Skillful and diplomatic missionaries, such as those who have worked in San Miguel Ixtahuacán and San Pedro, can promote ritual reorganization by encouraging dissidents, protecting them from conservative pressures, and by offering alternatives to native beliefs. Like all ritual organizations, however, the fiesta system is an adjustive mechanism that provides people with identity, social discipline, and a sense of spiritual security. As long as this mechanism works (in the sense that the bulk of its participants find it satisfying), it can resist intrusive ideologies. And when it no longer fulfills people's needs, especially when changing economies transform it into an economic burden, the fiesta system can collapse even in the absence of direct missionization. The missionary's role appears to be a facilitative one. He is the agent of acculturation, who gives form to new religious activities, but his success is conditioned to a large degree by the setting into which he walks (DeWalt 1975:96).

It thus seems reasonable to assume that the fiesta systems of Petz and Cucho have been preserved primarily by the economic resources that have allowed these communities to maintain productive and social independence in the face of population growth. Two resources are of major importance: their superior soils relative to those of the interior mountains, and their access to the land and markets of the Pacific lowlands.

As in San Miguel, people in Petz and Cucho are aware that population growth is threatening their traditional economy. *"Ahora es peublo,"* says a man from Petz, gesturing to the housetops poking up through the milpa to indicate that his aldea now seems more a town than a hamlet. A census of Petz done in 1968 by the aldean schoolteacher revealed 753 inhabitants, of whom fully 41 percent were under 15 years of age. Twenty-seven Indian mothers surveyed in Cucho have given birth to a total of 256 children, with mothers 45 years old and younger having an average of 4.3 living children, and mothers over 45 years of age having 4.8 living children. These statistics are comparable to those of San Miguel, and are underlain by identical processes.

As in San Miguel, population growth has had direct, locally recognized effects on the size of landholdings. Both Petz and Cucho are located on small plains, islands of flat land that jut out of a mountain ridge into a huge ravine opening to the Pacific coast. Behind them the land rises steeply up the ridge, and on all other sides it falls sharply into the ravine (see Map 3). The flat plains are still the communities' primary agricultural resource, but through time this land has been divided and redivided so that presently few families in either village can subsist from plains land alone.

Men commonly remark that the local land situation has degenerated since the time of their fathers. The *alcalde auxiliar* of Petz explained that although his father kept five cows and four mules, he himself would have difficulty maintaining such a herd due to scarcity of pasture. Land on the plain is now more completely sown in wheat and corn, the surrounding barrancos provide little natural forage, and the price of animal fodder has risen steeply. To check these impressions, I made a survey of generational chance in landholdings in Cucho, identical to the San Miguel survey. Sampling 29 Indian farmers, I found they own a total of 891 cuerdas while their fathers owned a total of 1346 cuerdas, a per capita decline of 16 cuerdas. Four fathers owned 100 cuerdas or more, but only one son owns this amount. (Land also appears to have been more unevenly distributed in the previous generation; there are more large holdings in the sample of fathers, and four men reported their fathers had owned no land at all.)

The land situation has not affected Petz and Cucho, however, nearly so severely as it has San Miguel. The people of these communities have larger incomes than do the Miguelenses, and earn these more easily in their own enterprises. Houses in Petz and Cucho are more ample than in San Miguel, and people are generally better clothed. There is also greater commercial elaboration in these communities. Cucho is dotted with Indian-owned shops, and there are eight small establishments in Petz, mostly tiny stores. A number of Indians in both communities have installed motor-driven corn mills in their homes, a significant investment since these mills cost between Q600 and Q700 when paid for on time. There are two corn mills in Petz, as many as in the entire municipio of San Miguel with its tenfold larger population. (Significantly, neither of the Miguelense mills is owned by a local Indian. The owner of one is a Ladino craftsman, the other belongs to an immigrant San Pedrano.) Domestic budgets of families in Petz and Cucho also tend to be larger than those of the Miguelenses, and less is spent to compensate for corn deficits. Even though they have fewer animals than did their parents, farmers in these two villages are more amply stocked than Miguelense *agricultores*. Cattle, especially, are much more prevalent in Petz and Cucho.

The primary evidence for the greater prosperity of Petz and Cucho is the uncommonness of the proletarian pattern of life among their members. Few people in Petz or Cucho engage in plantation labor in order to earn wages with which to purchase food. The percentage of residents who work on the fincas is much lower than in San Miguel, those who do this work tend to work fewer jornales per year than in San Miguel, and the pattern of participation is different. Only men and grown boys go to the plantations to work, and they go as free agents. No truckers come to haul the community off *en masse*, and there are no habilitadores in eight village. The need for coastal work among people of these two communities is too low to warrant these measures. I investigated wage work and corn purchasing among 48 Indian families, 19 from Petz and 29 from Cucho. Only 14 of these (29 percent) reported a member doing finca labor the previous year, averaging 73 jornales each. Three men, all from Cucho, performed 100 jornales or more, one man spending almost the entire year. The others sold between 16 and 60 days' labor to the plantations.

I found that 12 of these 48 men had sold surplus corn the previous year, and that another 11 neither sold nor purchased corn. Forty-eight percent of the sample, then, raised at least enough of the basic staple to sustain their families throughout the year. None of these men had done wage labor the year before. The rest of the men in the sample (25) had purchased corn the previous year, but half of them did so as an investment, rather than for direct subsistence. One was a carpenter who purchased corn when it was cheap in order to pay workers when the price rose. Others had pigs or milk cattle that consumed much corn, and one had 60 chickens to feed. Only 11 men out of the two-community sample, 23 percent of the total, displayed the San Miguel pattern of depending on corn purchased with harvest wages for the basic subsistence of their families.

The peasant prosperity in these communities can be attributed in part to their flat and productive land. Local soils produce continually with only the application of wastes and manure, and they produce well by highland standards. Farmers consistently report yields of one and a half to two quintals per cuerda; land used to graze animals for six months will produce over two quintales per cuerda.

As population has grown over the last generation, farmers have been pushing out onto marginal land on the slopes behind the villages and in the surrounding barrancos. They have not been forced, however, to rely exclusively on this land, since many rent land on the hot, fertile coast. Just as most Miguelenses travel to the coast each year to harvest other men's crops, many men from Petz and Cucho trek down the escarpment to cultivate and harvest their own. *La costa es lo que más ayuda aquí*, one man put it (the coast is our greatest help).

Coastal land is rented from large landowners, usually Ladinos, who own surpluses. The standard rent is 25 pounds of corn per cuerda of land, plus a few days' labor at harvest time for a minimum wage. Because the coast is hotter and wetter than the highlands, it yields two corn crops per year. As groups, the farmers hire trucks to carry their harvest back up to Cucho where they shuttle it to their houses with mules. Recently, many men in both communities have also purchased small coffee orchards, which they cultivate as semicommercial enterprises, selling a few quintals of good beans and consuming the rest.

This exploitation of coast land has been increasing. Adult men in Cucho say that when they were young few men planted corn on the coast, and those who did rented fields close by in El Quetzal, the piedmont community that borders on their home municipio. Nowadays greater numbers of men cultivated coastal corn (and coffee), and they are forced to go much farther down the coast to find available land. Twenty-three out of 30 men interviewed in Cucho had engaged in some coastal agriculture the preceding year, but only 10 of these men had fathers who cultivated corn or coffee on the coast at any time in their lives. Of 19 men interviewed in Petz, 15 had coastal interests. Of the 38 men engaged in coastal agriculture in the two-community sample, 9 cultivated coffee only, 17 corn only, and 12 both coffee and corn. The preceding year they had worked a total of 246 cuerdas of corn (two crops) and 156 cuerdas of coffee.

The people of these communities, unlike their Indian brethren in San Miguel, have not been experiencing a land shortage per se. Throughout their history they have enjoyed access to sufficient land, but recently they have had to walk farther to reach it. People in Petz and Cucho have also adapted to their land problem by becoming traders. Of the 30 men in the Cucho agricultural survey above, 13 are regular coastal traders, while only five had fathers who were in this business. Five of the 19 men in the Petz survey are also coastal traders. These men produce and buy highland specialties, such as sausages, vegetables, fruits, and cheeses, and pack them down to the coast on mules. Less often, they bring back coastal products to sell in the highlands. They make profits of between Q1.50 and Q4.00 per week from this activity.

Mules were previously the basis of commerce in the entire department, with the biggest traders (who often had large strings of animals) coming from San Pedro. As San Pedrano trade became mechanized, it posed a real threat to the smaller peddlers from outlying hamlets. San Pedro traders now communally rent trucks, carry goods to coastal markets in bulk, and sell at prices the muleteers cannot meet. To counter this competition, the peddlers of Petz and Cucho have shifted from selling in coastal plazas to selling directly on the fincas, where they can charge slightly higher prices and develop steady clients.

Comparing Petz and Cucho with the municipio of San Miguel Ixtahuacán, we find that the three communities have certain basic economic similarities underlain by a number of critical differences:

Capital situation. All three communities employ stagnant, archaic productive techniques to scratch income out of diminishing per capita resources. None is modernizing its economy at any appreciable rate, and in San Miguel a critical element of traditional technology (swidden fallowing) is no longer feasible. Population growth in Petz and Cucho has been cushioned by the richness of local resources and is compensated for by expanded exploitation of peripheral resources. San Miguel has no such peripheral resources, so people have been forced to cope with population pressure by selling their labor.

Control over means of production. As their economic dilemma intensified, Miguelenses lost more and more control over their labor, a process exacerbated by their lack of political power. Although the seasonal wage work pattern is definitely established in Petz and Cucho, the great majority of people are still their own bosses.

Market relations. The people of Petz and Cucho produce a small surplus of foods which, along with their services as peddlers, they sell in the regional market. Their status in the market is one of shared weakness. The market is atomistic. They have no particular power in it but neither are they threatened by large enterprise. Miguelenses, in contrast, produce insufficient food and must sell surplus labor, which exposes them to the much greater power of the finqueros. They are also more vulnerable to price inflation, since, relative to Petz and Cucho, they sell less and buy more (especially food), and have no control over that significant proportion of their income, wages.

In Petz and Cucho people are economically more comfortable than in San Miguel, while at the same time they are minimally involved in the economic expansion of San Pedro. They occupy a middle position, suffering no significant decline and enjoying no cumulative affluence. Conspicuous giving, consequently, is still a tenable activity.

FOURTEEN

Ethnicity, Power, and Culture Change in Mesoamerica

I have discussed a series of communities in western Guatemala and southeastern Mexico that share certain fundamental similarities. All are situated in the high mountains. All are Maya in their cultural and linguistic origins. All carry on significant household agriculture, but at the same time maintain important relations with the coastal and cash sectors of national economies. Here the basic likenesses end. Despite many similarities of history and structure, the villages and towns I visited are remarkably diversified in their sense of ethnic identity, their cultural orientations, and especially in their economic adaptations.

The purpose of this concluding chapter is to review the principal cases to identify the factors behind this diversification. My approach assumes that the current circumstances of Indian communities must be understood as consequences of the historical interplay of local resources with larger forces of a political nature that originate beyond the Indian sector. Four factors emerge in this analysis as especially relevant. The two most important of these are demographic factors (the growth and distribution of local populations), and national economic factors (infrastructure development and the need for Indian labor and products in national economies). These factors are basic because their effects are so pervasive. All the communities studied have in some way been profoundly influenced by demographic expansion and by major currents in the political economies of Mexico and Guatemala. Also significant are geographic factors (location of communities in relation to markets and agricultural land), and strategic decisions by national political and religious organizations that bear directly on Indian communities.

This approach to the social structure of Mesoamerican society differs from other current approaches that emphasize ethnic ideals and national ideologies as determining conditions. The new wave of plural society analyses, for example, go beyond the limited focus of earlier community studies, but they share with these studies a similar concern for mental culture, and so tend to neglect crucial structural factors (Goldkind 1963, Wasserstrom 1975). Colby and van den Berghe's interpretation of ethnic "passing" in Mesoamerican societies is very similar to the functionalist explanations we have discussed in its underemphasis of the economics of ethnicity and its overemphasis of cultural perceptions and ideals (Smith 1975). Their explanation of why ethnic passing is more common in Chiapas than in Guatemala relies heavily on such factors as Mexico's long-standing assimilationist "policy," and on the greater "consciousness" and "dichotomous view" of ethnicity that they believe prevails in Guatemala (1961:788). Elsewhere Colby and van den Berghe add that since Ladinos in both Chiapas and Guatemala generally are in favor of assimilating Indians into national life, much of the explanation for the firmer Guatemalan ethnic line "must be found in characteristics of the Indian group itself." The Indian characteristics they specify are also cultural modes. Basing their argument on the Ixil, they maintain that passing is uninteresting to Guatemalan Indians because they can obtain Ladino material objects without changing their identity, and because other aspects of Ladino culture "are perceived as alien and undesirable." Ixil culture, furthermore, stresses group solidarity and "harmonious social order" rather than the kind of individual self-assertiveness that in Chiapas promotes passing (Colby and van den Berghe 1969:177-79).

This plural society approach is slanted toward ideology, since it is only in this realm that Mesoamerican societies are in any way "plural" (Frank 1967; Stavenhagen 1968b). Although Colby and van den Berghe designate national political and economic structures as the "core" of the plural society, their definitions and interpretations stress the symbolic differences between Indian and Ladino groups—differences in cosmology, language, kin patterns, dress styles and so on—much more than economic competition, conflict, and the domination of one ethnic group by another (1969:7, 20). National political and economic institutions are viewed less as means of social control than as "integrative and cohesive factors" that allow segmented plural societies to "hang together." Their special concern for ethnic passing as the major process of change in contemporary Mesoamerica confirms their emphasis on ideology, since passing is achieved largely by the assumption of out-group symbolic culture (see van den Berghe 1968; Colby and van den Berghe 1969:91-92, 179).

The effects of cultural bias are even more pronounced in Collier's recent study of land and ethnicity in Chiapas (1975). *Environment* is the guiding concept in Collier's "ecological" analysis of Tzotzil culture. "Rather than attributing the tradition of Tzotzil tribes to their isolation," he says, "we attribute it to their environment" (1975:3). Collier encounters the environment by building his study from the local level upward, but as he proceeds from questions of land rental and Zinacanteco kinship organization to broader questions of colonialism and land reform, his conception of the environment increasingly emphasizes symbolic features. This shift from the material aspect to the ideological aspect of the environment creates a double vision in Collier's work, a split between the facts he reports and his interpretation of these facts. This double vision is most apparent in his discussion of the key issue of land reform.

In Collier's view, agrarian movements play a pivotal role in sustaining Tzotzil tribal identity, while at the same time promoting broader, national sentiments. His analysis of Indian agrarianism is wholly optimistic, stressing the political effectiveness of what he calls Indian "blocs," and the creativity and drive of Indian political leaders. Local agrarian movements, to begin with, have been "spurred by nationalist agrarian ideology." These movements then in turn solidify tribal identity be securing and improving the Indians' land base, and simultaneously promote among the Indians a "civil" or national consciousness. National land reform ideology, in Collier's analysis, is a key initiating factor in the environment that is promoting both material progress and a sense of national involvement among the Indians of Chiapas:

> As a nationalist ideology and an economic policy, land reform has reached down to the remotest corner of the nation and into the consciousness of the natives. And the leaders of these natives have drawn upon land reform to better the land base of their constituencies. Their awareness of land reform ideology inspires native groups to take action at the local level to better their resource bases. . . . Land reform, a nationally based program, cannot be ignored as an element in the environment of local land use (1975:6).

What is missing from this analysis, so focused on sentimental integration, is any strong sense of the crisis, polarization, and conflict that also accompany agrarian movements. Collier's principal example of recent Indian activism, for example, is built around a trip he took to the state capital along with eight Zinacantecos who were pressing a claim to a parcel of hot-country

land. Although the lawyer they were scheduled to meet missed the appointment and managed to stay a step ahead as they pursued him through the day,
Collier is most impressed with the Indians' understanding of the situation, and
with their dogged determination, which "almost had overcome the notorious
languor of the Mexican bureaucracy" (1975:201).

We should be all the more impressed to learn that these Zinancantecos
and their kin have been pressing their right to colonize this hot-country parcel
with similar zeal and determination (but without complete success) ever since
they purchased it in 1908. Over this period the Indians have been in constant
confrontation with equally determined Ladino ranchers who have doctored
land titles and bribed officials to legalize their encroachment on Indian
property. Collier's ingenuous interpretation of this legal barricading is that the
Indian colonizers' ultimate success will have the positive effect of solidifying
their tribal identity, while integrating them into modern society by engender-
ing "a civil consciousness like that Geertz sees springing initially from
primordial consciousness of kind" (1975:202).

This is certainly making the best of a bad bargain. Just how bad this
bargain is on a regional scale is made clear in Collier's description of the
impact of population growth on Indian subsistence agriculture. Population
pressure, we learn from this book, is so severe that large sections of the
highland landscape are eroded and rural people have been forced to seek new
sources of land and income. Climax forest remains in the highlands only
where agriculture is impossible. Eighty percent of the Zinacanteco corn
harvest now comes from hot-country enterprises, even though lowland farming generates less return to investment than highland agriculture, and requires
Zinacanteco farmers to rent land from Ladino ranchers. Chamula is hardest hit
of all the Tzotzil municipios, as Collier shows in a chapter on soil erosion.
Heavy pressure has forced Chamulas into intensive horticulture and other
farm practices that he claims further degrade their damaged landscape. They
are also increasingly dependent on cottage industries and wage labor to
supplement farm income.

Given this description, we must be skeptical of Collier's explanation that
the Indians' growing agrarian excitement is stimulated from above by the
diffusion of Indianist land reform "ideology." We must also be skeptical
when he insists that Indian land politics is successfully securing the Indian's
land situation. In the broad view, Collier's brand of ideological environmen-
talism owes more to Redfield than to Darwin (not to mention Marx) and is out
of phase with his documentation.

Collier's approach, and that of Colby and van den Berghe, represents an effort to see beyond the limits of single-community functionalism. This asset aside, their shared emphasis on cultural ideals, on social integration over social conflict, and on differences over inequalities demonstrates that this effort is the extension of conventional ethnological concerns under the guise of new terminologies.

Mesoamerican ethnology needs comprehensive approaches such as these, but even more it needs an approach that emphatically recognizes that the social environment is stratified and that its components are grossly unequal in privileges, wealth, and, most important, power. We need a "political ecology" that sets out the political economy of the nation as the broadest frame of analysis, then studies the adaptations of regional and local societies to this frame. The following analysis of the cases used in the present study was developed with these ideas in mind.

The history of San Miguel Ixtahuacán shows that even in this isolated corner of Guatemala, the institutional integration of local society with the outside world has progressed considerably in recent decades. Dependence on wage work and cash have increased as the native subsistence economy faltered under the dense Indian population. Crusading churches, uninvited but not entirely unwelcomed, attacked the area as a religious frontier. Since the Ubico period and the Revolution of 1944, the locality has been more closely incorporated into national politics, never reestablishing its earlier gerontocratic structure. There have been some improvements in schools, roads, and marketplaces. If we compare San Miguel Ixtahuacán today to the same community before the Ubico-Revolution episode, it is now somewhat less isolated (there are radios and buses, people understand more Spanish, and there are more institutional connections with modern society), somewhat more differentiated (political and religious organizations are more complex and open), and considerably more dependent on outside products (food, clothing). Despite these alterations, much of Indian culture remains strong in this municipio. Most Miguelenses still speak Mam, dress in a style that is distinctly Indian, and identify themselves as "naturales."

Changes in San Pedro, by contrast, have been more pervasive. In this centrally located community many overt signs of Indianness have been shrugged off as the town has become entrepreneurial, literate, and tightly involved with national markets and groups. This process has entailed considerable assimilation of national culture, including radical modernization of consumer preferences and religious values. San Pedro's Indianness remains primarily in its heritage and in the lingering Indian identity of its inhabitants. With the exception of these traits, the community is rapidly becoming an effective participant in modern Guatemalan life.

Economically, Petz and Cucho appear to be a kind of midpoint between San Miguel Ixtahuacán's dependence and the emerging capitalism of San Pedro. Because they are more successfully self-sufficient, these villages have less to do with outside people or their culture, and the weakness of outside influence explains their cultural conservatism. The recent experience of Petz and Cucho in many ways parallels that of Zinacantán, discussed in chapter 4. These communities share the good fortune of having easy access to urban markets and to hot-country land. This has allowed them to intensify trade and extend their milpas over new land, which has softened the effects of their population growth. Thus retaining their subsistence autonomy, Petz, Cucho, and Zinacantán have also preserved their social insularity and local identities. Their strong subsistence economies also provide the surpluses that allow them to continue expressing this identity through religious feasting and ceremonial sponsorship.

The extensive changes in San Miguel and San Pedro are not so easily explained, although here, too, the interplay of local and national factors is clear. San Miguel is particularly vulnerable to outside forces precisely because it has so few resources. It is isolated in the interior mountains, its soils are shallow and steep, it has few sources of nonagricultural income other than plantation work, and its farm technology is antiquated and ineffective. Compared even to traditional Indian communities such as Petz, Cucho, and Zinacantán, Miguelenses have relatively little to work with. They also suffer from the general Indian liability of being politically isolated, since there are no larger organizations that represent them as Indians, farmers, or workers. This latter fact is especially important, because it exposes the Miguelenses to the much greater power of national coffee and cotton interests (see Dessaint 1962; Hoyt 1955). The thousands of seasonal plantation workers in Guatemala have no effective union, so, in the historic Mesoamerican pattern, they are much weaker than their numbers would imply. Protective legislation has done little to ease this situation. Indians are too poor to hire lawyers or to lose employment in fighting abuses, and the labor inspectors and judges appointed to protect them are overworked, underpaid, and susceptible to corruption (Adams 1970:425-32). The plantation owners, who thwarted the Arbenz land reform, and who, as a tiny fraction of the population, own virtually all the nation's prime farmland, dominate their laborers totally (Adams 1970:396ff; Colby and van den Berghe 1969:34-35).

The lack of a comprehensive program to develop highland agriculture also contributes to San Miguel's depressed position. Although La Labor Ovalle, an experimental farm near Quezaltenango, has produced advanced strains of high-altitude wheat and corn, the agricultural extension and credit facilities for transmitting these advances to the campesinos are poorly developed. There is only one government extension agent in the entire highlands of San Marcos, responsible for 17 dispersed and isolated townships. The National Wheat Growers' Union has only two officials in this region. These are common problems throughout the Indian regions of Guatemala. While surveying the entire highlands, Hill and Gollas "rarely encountered" either agricultural credit facilities or extension agents (1968:45).

It might be argued that these facilities are scarce because there is no demand for them among Indian farmers. The weakness of agrarian politics in San Miguel, however, obscures in an unfortunate way the interest that many Indians have in improving their farms. No Indian I know in Petz, Cucho, or any of the villages of San Miguel Ixtahuacán has ever heard of La Labor Ovalle, and many are unaware of the Wheat Growers' Union. There is, consequently, little organized pressure to expand these facilities. Most men nevertheless are curious about agriculture, and respond eagerly to new ideas. When I invited an agronomist to lecture in a Miguelense aldea, 70 men attended, all of them Indian campesinos. Many of these were persuaded to dig contour ditches to protect fields from erosion, despite the heavy work involved.

The underdevelopment of Indian agriculture thus seems to stem more from national politics than from local disinterest. In general, highland agriculture is simply neglected, and at times the government even acts directly contrary to its welfare. During the 1970 presidential elections, Partido Revolucionario, the party in power, attempted to use the National Wheat Growers' Union as a campaign agency. Before the elections, Union field representatives were pressured into distributing PR literature among their clients, and for a period the government actually intervened in the organization, replacing the director with its own agent for fabricated reasons. The Union is a private, strictly nonpolitical organization that, however understaffed and underfunded, provides the most visible agricultural development service in the Indian region. Political manuvering weakens the Union by disrupting its activities and threatening the morale of its field agents, who are forced to lay their jobs on the line by publicly advocating, or refusing to advocate, a political party.

The government's general lack of interest in the agrarian crisis of San Miguel and other highland communities stems, however, from deeper considerations. Agricultural expansion in the Indian sector would inevitably drive up the price of coffee labor, which would threaten government revenues as well as the income of the nation's most powerful elite.

The growing incorporation of San Miguel into the cash sector may also be contributing to the community's rapid population growth, since it is possible that the additional demands of wage labor on the already hard-working Indian family may promote high fertility (see White 1973 for such an analysis of Java's population growth). Whatever is provoking San Miguel's demographic explosion, the government is doing little to dampen it, either through medical services or by investing in the kinds of social development that would reduce the Indians' desire for many children. In the short run this policy, or lack of it, will benefit certain sectors of of the Guatemalan economy by making Indian labor cheaper and easier to control. In the long run it can only create social problems of the greatest magnitude. These problems have already appeared in San Miguel, where the severity of basic economic need has locked the community into a downward spiral of congestion, market dependence, and agricultural decline.

On top of the economic absorption of this previously isolated community, outside forces have reordered life in San Miguel through strategic decisions. First the intendentes, then political parties and elected municipal administration were imposed on San Miguel by national governments. The recent wave of missionization, another outside force, also crashed down on them from above, and helped push Miguelenses a step closer to the mainstream of Guatemalan institutional life. These strategic actions, however, have had little effect on the community's cultural orientation, because they are unaccompanied by effective economic developments. (Plantation labor has had the major consequence of breaking down the community's subsistence economy, without pulling it into meaningful new social relationships that would reduce its insularity or alter its identity.) The conjunction of these factors has produced the San Miguel we see today, a community that is to some degree less isolated and more differentiated, and to a large degree more dependent than it ever was in its peasant past. But it has also produced a community that is still Indian in virtually every way, except for losing the traditional rituals that would supposedly preserve its Indianness.

The recent situation of San Miguel is similar in many ways to that of Chamula, since in both these communities population growth and soil erosion have exacerbated subsistence problems. Lacking direct access to hot-country land, many Miguelenses and Chamulas solve these problems through seasonal plantation labor. In San Miguel, however, the economic reverses associated with plantation labor have been so severe that they have already caused a reduction in traditional religious spending. This does not appear to be the case in Chamula (Gossen 1974:13-14), perhaps because Chamula enjoys several economic advantages that San Miguel lacks. Since Chamula is not nearly so isolated as San Miguel, some Chamulas do find it feasible to rent and work hot country land (Gossen 1974:7). Chamula, furthermore, is close to the urban market of San Cristóbal, and has a complex of handicraft specialties—pine furniture, pottery, charcoal, and so on—that provide considerable income (Collier 1975:122). San Miguel has no such market connection and few handicraft specialties. Plantation laborers also seem to be better paid in Mexico than in Guatemala—on this point it is interesting that many Guatemalan Indians prefer to work on Mexican fincas. Chamula's native religion, we should also note, has not come under nearly the same missionary pressure as that of San Miguel. The orthodox Church is so weak in Chamula that the Ladino priest is not even allowed to spend the night in the municipio.

San Pedro presents a radically different picture from any of the other communities. San Pedro is still identified as an Indian community, and still recognizes its own Indianness, but beneath this cloak of identity, San Pedranos are avid students and entrepreneurs who are speedily adopting national culture. Why is San Pedro modernizing so rapidly? And why, of all communities in the region, is San Pedro alone making this rapid transformation?

Here again, the interplay of national and local conditions provides the key. Using all the cases available, it seems that three factors are necessary to explain Indian economic development in San Pedro. These are the general growth of Guatemala's economic infrastructure, the productive vitality of the Indian family, and the large, concentrated population of the San Pedro community. None of these factors by itself provides a complete account, but together they shed considerable light on San Pedro's unusual and rapid growth.

Infrastructure development played a seminal role in San Pedro's growth. The roads, trucks, markets, and schools that the community now exploits so fully were not there a few decades ago. Many other highland communities, however, have similar access to roads and schools but have not modernized to the degree that San Pedro has. Sometimes communities that are closest to the very centers of public investment are the most traditional and conservative of all—Chamula, on the outskirts of San Cristóbal, is such a case. Although San Pedro benefited from its proximity to the departmental capital, the availability of new capital alone is not the answer.

San Pedranos have also benefited in an ironic way from their historical status as a preindustrial farming and trading community, which is a second critical factor. San Pedranos presently dominate regional commerce in large part because their historic labor-intensive niche promoted among them an economically efficient family. The Ladino merchants of San Marcos are in trouble because they are competing with an ethnic group whose traditional family organization is economically superior to their own. Ladino businessmen uniformly fear their Indian competitors because, as one Quezaltenango Ladino put it, of the Indians' willingness to live "below their means," while Ladinos in their middle-class way must live above theirs. As they enter the early stages of development, Indian entrepreneurs commonly maintain their customary standard of living, deferring improvements in diet, clothing, and housing in favor of reinvestment. Compared to Ladinos, furthermore, Indian children become productive at a tender age, and Indian wives—unlike their Ladina counterparts, who are commonly unemployed and demand household help besides—strap their babies on their backs and set about their trades and crafts. Indian families also tend to keep in close touch with their operations, rather than allocating the harder and more routine tasks to unreliable help, as Ladinos often do. The dynamic Indian household thus generates more income, allocates a greater proportion to capital investment, and can undercut its Ladino competition at will. "The Ladino," one San Pedrano reflected, "wants to earn too much. He can't compete with the *muchachos.*"

Indian culture thus has its areas of competitive strength as well as "liabilities" such as the fiesta system. These strengths and liabilities, however, are universals, as broadly distributed as the Indians themselves, so their expression must depend on local economic circumstances. To develop and become competitive with Ladinos, Indian communities must control a third resource, the very one they have most conspicuously lacked throughout their colonial history. This resource is a strong base of coordinated productive power. Being similar in broad outline, the recent histories of San Pedro and Quezaltenango show how this power emerges in certain Indian communities.

Economic development among Quezalteco Indians is perhaps even more impressive than that of San Pedranos. Colby and van den Berghe note the mercantile expansion of these Indians, and their considerable wealth

(1961:787). Hupp finds that most Indians in Quezaltenango fall into a broad middle class of shopkeepers and artisans, with a minority of poor and another of rich (1966). The wealthiest Indians are richer than most Ladinos in Quezaltenango, and there is significant upward mobility in the Indian ranks. Many Indian businesses have moved into the central business district of the town. In 1969 I surveyed this district, finding that about a third of its stores were owned by Ladinos, a third by immigrants, and a third by Indians. Cultural changes in Quezaltenango have also paralleled those of San Pedro, with major alterations in consumption patterns and religious activity. It is true that Quezaltenango Indians, faced with a resident and resistant Ladino community, have preserved their native language and women's garb much more than the San Pedranos, but these are relatively unimportant cultural survivals compared to the major changes they have experienced in other areas of life. Besides, most Quezaltecos are also fluent in Spanish, and the women often wear nylon stockings and high heels with their Indian skirts.

This rapid growth in the Indian economy accompanied by integration with national culture has occurred in San Pedro and Quezaltenango primarily because both these communities are towns rather than villages. Beings towns, they were "preadapted," in a sense, for economic growth when such opportunities presented themselves. It is easier for Indians to coalesce and exert economic power where they form a concentrated group of 10,000, as in San Pedro, or 24,000, as in Quezaltenango. With their large and concentrated populations these two communities could, and did, overcome the power disadvantages suffered by dispersed Indian settlements such as those of the interior mountains of San Marcos, or of highland Chiapas.

The advantages of a large concentrated population begin at the basic economic level of specialization of labor. In Mesoamerica, the common village pattern is for each community to specialize in some craft such as weaving or pottery as a part-time adjunct to horticulture, and to exchange its specialty with other villages in a regional or "solar" market system. San Pedro, in contrast, was by itself able to support a variety of full-time specialists even before development, because the demand for crafts was sufficient to induce some men to engage in them virtually full time. San Pedro carpenters, for example, are so renowned that I have encountered them working on contract over 30 miles from home. Textile industries have grown in San Pedro in part because a round trip to Guatemala City can now be made in one day, while in the 1930s it took most of a week. But while rapid travel has become generally available to many rural communities, San Pedro had the developed skills to exploit it. Also, these skills were available in a thickly settled urban labor force that could be easily coordinated into "putting-out" firms.

Large Indian communities, furthermore, have the strength of numbers to penetrate Ladino schools. Ladinos have never been able to frighten Indians away from San Marcos schools, because the Indians attend "en fuerza." The first secondary school opened in San Marcos in the mid-1940s to immediate, large, Indian enrollments. San Marcos now has four secondaries. All have significant Indian enrollments and in one Indians are the majority.

A final and highly significant advantage of size is that many educated San Pedranos settle in their native town to live and work, which rarely happens in villages. The occasional educated villager is usually drawn away to the bright lights and opportunities of larger cities—a form of human "decapitalization" that is one of the many ways in which large communities sap the strength of their hinterlands (Stavenhagen 1968b). San Pedro suffers less from urban talent drain because it is large enough to support a literate class. The white-collar elite of San Pedro is civically active and is largely responsible for establishing the night schools, leading the various betterment committees, and providing the sophisticated political leadership that makes this community so unusual. (San Pedro, for example, is one of the few Indian communities in Guatemala that always has a mayor who can read.) San Pedranos who have moved to Guatemala City are also not entirely lost, since there are enough of them to provide national-level political influence by acting as an organized community lobby.

Vigorous family organization, in conjunction with expanding commercial opportunities and a strong, concentrated population, have allowed San Pedro to break the constraints that hem in small Indian villages. The benefits of a concentrated, highly organized population, added to its central location, allowed San Pedro to mitigate the common problems of population pressure, *minifundismo* and dependence on plantation labor through the elaboration of nonagrarian industries and commerce. This development then promoted the rapid cultural modernization that lifted the town to its premier position in regional life.

San Pedro's major advantage is that it is not a tiny spot squatting at the edge of a regional capital; it is the largest community in its area. Relative to the villages surrounding it, the economy of San Pedro has always been more dynamic and complex. As new economic opportunities appeared, San Pedro was most able to shrug off its liabilities and adapt. Now, controlling a modern educational and economic base and led by a literate elite, it has entered a phase of self-sustaining growth. At present, it is even showing signs of itself becoming a "colonial city," since many of its traders and truckers now thirve off of interior markets. But although the dependency of communities like San Miguel results in profits for San Pedro, San Pedro differs from classic colonial cities because it is attached to its hinterland with ties of kinship and common ethnic heritage. Because its economy is growing and it is not protecting a stagnant colonial niche, San Pedro also tends to be less dominating and exploitative than other regional giants.

Bibliography

Adams, Richard N. (ed.)
1957 *Political changes in Guatemalan Indian communities: A symposium*. New Orleans: Middle American Research Institute.

Adams, Richard Newbold
1970 *Crucifixion by power: Essays on Guatemalan national social structure, 1944-1966*. Austin: University of Texas Press.

Barnard, Chester I.
1966 *The functions of the executive*. Cambridge: Harvard University Press.

Barrett, Jon H.
1970 *Individual goals and organizational objectives: A study of integration mechanisms*. Ann Arbor: Center for Research on Utilization of Scientific Knowledge.

Bunzel, Ruth
1967 *Chichicastenango: A Guatemalan village*. Seattle: University of Washington Press.

Cancian, Francesca
1960 Functional analysis of change. *American Sociological Review* 25:818-27.

Cancian, Frank
1963 Informant error and native prestige ranking in Zinacantan. *American Anthropologist* 65:1068-1075.
1965 *Economics and prestige in a Maya community: The religious cargo system of Zinacantan*. Stanford: Stanford University Press.

1972   *Change and uncertainty in a peasant economy: The Maya corn farmers of Zinacantan.* Stanford: Stanford University Press.

Colby, Benjamin N., and Pierre L. van den Berghe
1961   Ethnic relations in southeastern Mexico. *American Anthropologist* 63:772-92.
1969   *Ixil country: A plural society in the highlands of Guatemala.* Berkeley: University of California Press.

Collier, George A.
1975   *Fields of the Tzotzil: The ecological bases of tradition in highland Chiapas.* Austin: University of Texas Press.

Consuegra, Sfelino
n.d.   *Monografía del municipio de San Pedro Sacatepéquez.* Departamento de San Marcos, Guatemala.

Dessaint, Alain X.
1962   Effects of the hacienda and plantation systems on Guatemala's Indians. *América Indígena* 22:323-54.

DeWalt, Billie R.
1975   Changes in the cargo systems of Mesoamerica. *Anthropological Quarterly* 48:87-105.

Epstein, T.S.
1962   *Economic development and social change in south India.* Manchester: The University Press.

Erasmus, Charles J.
1961   *Man takes control: Cultural development and American aid.* Minneapolis: University of Minnesota Press.
1967   Upper limits of peasantry and agrarian reform. *Ethnology* 6:349-80.
1968   Community development and the encogido syndrome. *Human Organization* 27:65-94.

Favre, Henri
1973   *Cambio y continuidad entre los mayas de Mexico.* México, D.F.: Siglo Veintiuno Editores.

Flannery, Kent V.
1972   The cultural evolution of civilization. *Annual Review of Ecology and Systematics* 3:399-426.

Frank, Andre Gunder
1967 *Capitalism and underdevelopment in Latin America: Historical studies of Chile and Brazil.* New York: Monthly Review Press.

Goldkind, Victor
1963 Ethnic relations in southeastern Mexico: A methodological note. *American Anthropologist* 65:394-99.

Gossen, Gary H.
1974 *Chamulas in the world of the sun: Time and space in a Maya oral tradition.* Cambridge: Harvard University Press.

Goubaud Carrera, Antonio, Juan de Dios Rosales, and Sol Tax
1947 *Reconnaissance of northern Guatemala 1944.* Microfilm Collection of Manuscripts on Middle American Cultural Anthropology no. 17. Chicago: University of Chicago Library.

Gregg, Dorothy, and Elgin Williams
1948 The dismal science of functionalism. *American Anthropologist* 50:595-611.

Guiteras-Holmes, Calixta
1961 *Perils of the soul: The world view of a Tzotzil Indian.* New York: Free Press of Glencoe.

Harris, Marvin
1964 *Patterns of race in the Americas.* New York: Walker and Co.

Hempel, Carl G.
1959 The logic of functional analysis, in Llewellyn Gross (ed.), *Symposium on Sociological Theory.* White Plains, N.Y.: Row, Peterson and Co.

Hill, George W., and Manuel Gollas
1968 *The minifundia economy and society of the Guatemalan Indian.* Madison, Wisc.: Land Tenure Center.

Hinshaw, Robert E.
1975 *Panajachel: A Guatemalan town in thirty-year persepctive.* Pittsburgh: University of Pittsburgh Press.

Homans, George C.
1964 Bringing men back in. *American Sociological Review* 29:809-18.

Hoyt, Elizabeth E.
   1955   The Indian laborer on Guatemala's coffee fincas. *Inter-American Economic Affairs* 9:33-46.

Hupp, Bruce F.
   1966   The urban Indians of Quezaltenango, Guatemala. M.A. thesis, University of Texas.

James, Preston E.
   1969   *Latin America*. Indianapolis: Bobbs-Merrill Co.

Jones, Chester Lloyd
   1940   *Guatemala: Past and present*. Minneapolis: University of Minnesota Press.

Klein, Herbert S.
   1966   Peasant communities in revolt: The Tzeltal republic of 1712. *Pacific Historical Review* 35:247-63.

Leach, E. R.
   1965   *Political systems of highland Burma*. Boston: Beacon Press.

MacLeod, Murdo J.
   1973   *Spanish Central America: A socioeconomic history, 1520-1720*. Berkeley: University of California Press.

March, James G., and Herbert A. Simon
   1958   *Organizations*. New York: John Wiley & Sons.

Margolies, Luise Barbara
   1975   *Princes of the Earth; Subcultural diversity in a Mexican municipality*. Washington, D.C.: American Anthropological Association.

Mendelsohn, E. Michael
   1957   *Religion and world view in Santiago Atitlan*. Microfilm Collection of Manuscripts on American Indian Cultural Anthropology no. 52. Chicago: University of Chicago Library.

Murdock, George Peter
   1971   Anthropology's mythology. *Proceedings of the Royal Anthropological Institute of Great Britian and Ireland for 1971:* 17-24.

Nash, Manning
  1958 Political relations in Guatemala. *Social and Economic Studies* 7:65-75.
  1966 *Primitive and peasant economic systems.* San Francisco: Chandler Publishing Co.

Nuñez del Prado, Oscar
  1955 Aspects of Andean native life. *Kroeber Anthropological Society Papers* 12:1-21.

O'Neale, Lila M.
  1945 *Textiles of highland Guatemala.* Washington, D.C.: Carnegie Institution of Washington.

Pozas, Ricardo
  1952 El trabajo en las plantaciones de café y el cambio sociocultural del indio. *Revista Mexicana de Estudios Antropológicos* 13:31-48.

Radcliffe-Brown, A. R.
  1922 *The Andaman islanders.* Cambridge: Cambridge University Press.

Redfield, Robert
  1945 *Ethnographic materials on Agua Escondida.* Microfilm Collection of Manuscripts on Middle American Cultural Anthropology no. 3. Chicago: University of Chicago Library.

Reina, Ruben
  1966 *The law of the saints: A Pokomam pueblo and its community culture.* Indianapolis: Bobbs-Merrill Co.

Saler, Benson
  1971 Review of Evon Z. Vogt, Zinacantan: a Maya community in the highlands of Chiapas *American Anthropologist* 73:338-40.
  1972 A reply to Vogt. *American Anthropologist* 74:202.

Samayoa Chinchilla, Carlos
  1960 Notas sobre las causas que más influyeron en las derrotas de los ejércitos indígenas durante las guerras de conquista. *Antropología e Historia de Guatemala* 12:35-46.

Siverts, Henning
  1969 Ethnic stability and boundary dynamics in southern Mexico, in Frederik Barth (ed.), *The social organization of culture difference.* Boston: Little, Brown and Co.

Smelser, Neil
   1959   *Social change in the industrial revolution: An application of theory to the British cotton industry.* Chicago: University of Chicago Press.

Smith, Waldemar R.
   1975   Beyond the plural society: Economics and ethnicity in Middle American towns. *Ethnology* 14:225-44.

Stadelman, Raymond
   1940   *Maize cultivation in northwestern Guatemala.* Contributions to American Anthropology and History, vol. VI, no. 33. Carnegie Institution of Washington.

Stavenhagen, Rudolfo
   1968a   Classes, colonialism, and acculturation, in Joseph A. Kahl (ed.), *Comparative perspectives on stratification: Mexico, Great Britian, Japan.* Boston: Little, Brown and Co.
   1968b   Seven fallacies about Latin America, in James Petras and Maurice Zeitlan (eds.), *Latin America: Reform or revolution?* Greenwich: Fawcett Publications.

Stein, William H.
   1961   *Hualcan: Life in the highlands of Peru.* Ithaca: Cornell University Press.

Tax, Sol
   1937   The municipios of the midwestern highlands of Guatemala. *American Anthropologist* 39:423-44.
   1941   World view and social relations in Guatemala. *American Anthropologist* 43:27-42.
   1953   *Penny capitalism: A Guatemalan Indian economy.* Washington, D.C., Smithsonian Institution, Institute of Social Anthropology Publication no. 16.

Taylor, William B.
   1972   *Landlord and peasant in colonial Oaxaca.* Stanford: Stanford University Press.

van den Berghe, Gwendoline, and Pierre L. van den Berghe
   1966   Compadrazgo and class in southeastern Mexico. *American Anthropologist* 68:1236—44.

van den Berghe, Pierre L.
1968 Ethnic membership and cultural change in Guatemala. *Social Forces* 46:514-22.

van den Berghe, Pierre L., and Benjamin N. Colby
1961 Ladino-Indian relations in the highlands of Chiapas, Mexico. *Social Forces* 40:63-71.

Van Zantwijk, R. A. M.
1967 *Servants of the saints: The social and cultural identity of a Tarascan community in Mexico.* Assen, Netherlands: Royal VanGorcum.

Vogt, Evon Z.
1969 *Zinacantan: A Maya community in the highlands of Chiapas.* Cambridge: Belknap Press of Harvard University Press.
1972 Comment on Benson Saler's review of Zinacantan. *American Anthropologist* 74:201-2.

Wagley, Charles
1941 *Economics of a Guatemalan village.* Memoir no. 58, American Anthropological Association.
1949 *The social and religious life of a Guatemalan village.* Memoir no. 71, American Anthropological Association.

Wasserstrom, Robert
1974 The exchange of saints in Zinacantán. Paper presented at the XLI International Congress of Americanists, México, D.F., September 5, 1974.
1975 Revolution in Guatemala: Peasants and politics under the Arbenz government. *Comparative Studies in Society and History* 17:443-78.
1976 Land and labor in central Chiapas: A regional analysis. San Cristóbal de Las Casas: Centro de Investigaciones Ecológicas del Sureste.
n.d. End of the diaspora: Cattlemen and tenant farmers in central Chiapas, 1910-1973. Manuscript.

White, Benjamin
1973 Demand for labor and population growth in colonial Java. *Human Ecology* 1:217-36.

Wolf, Eric
   1955   Types of Latin American peasantry. *American Anthropologist* 57:452-71.
   1959   *Sons of the shaking earth*. Chicago: University of Chicago Press.
   1966   *Peasants*. Englewood Cliffs, Prentice-Hall.
   1967   The closed corporate community in Mesoamerica and central Java, in Jack M. Potter, May N. Diaz, and George M. Foster (eds.) *Peasant society: A reader*. Boston: Little, Brown and Co.

Index